## The First Americans

✶ ✶ ✶ ✶ ✶ ✶ ✶ ✶ ✶ ✶ ✶ ✶ ✶ ✶

# INDIANS OF THE SOUTHEAST

Richard E. Mancini

Facts On File, Inc.

AN INFOBASE HOLDINGS COMPANY

About *The First Americans* Series:

This eight-volume series presents the rich and varied cultures of the many Native American tribes, placing each within its geographical and historical context. Each volume covers a different cultural area, providing an understanding of all the major North American Indian tribes in a systematic, region-by-region survey. The series emphasizes the contributions of Native Americans to American culture, illustrating their legacy in striking photographs within the text and in all-color photo essays.

*Indians of the Southeast.*

Facts On File, Inc.
11 Penn Plaza
New York NY 10001

**Library of Congress Cataloging-in-Publication Data**

Mancini, Richard E.
    Indians of the Southeast / Richard E. Mancini
        p.    cm. — The First Americans series
    Includes index.
    Summary: Explores the ways of life of Native Americans of the
pre-colonial southeast United States, including tribal structure, language,
customs, and religion. Focuses on the Indians' planting of crops and
their contributions to agriculture.
    ISBN 0-8160-2390-5
    1. Indians of North America—Southeastern States—Juvenile literature.
[1. Indians of North America—Southeastern States.]
I. Title        II. Series.
E78.S65M29   1991
975' .00497—dc20                                        90—46543

Facts On File books are available at special discounts when purchased in bulk quantities for businesses, associations, institutions or sales promotions. Please call our Special Sales Department in New York at 212/967-8800 or 800/322-8755.

Design by Carmela Pereira
Jacket design by Donna Sinisgalli
Typography & composition by Tony Meisel
Manufactured by R. R. Donnelley & Sons
Printed in MEXICO

10 9 8 7 6 5 4 3 2

This book is printed on acid-free paper.

▲ Veteran Seminole carvers practice the age-old craft of creating a dugout canoe from a cypress tree during the Chalo Nitka Festival on Florida's Lake Okeechobee. The annual festival, whose name translates to "day of the bass," is a nine-week fishing tournament held between mid-January and early March.

# CONTENTS

✳ ✳ ✳ ✳ ✳ ✳ ✳ ✳ ✳ ✳ ✳ ✳ ✳

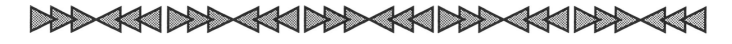

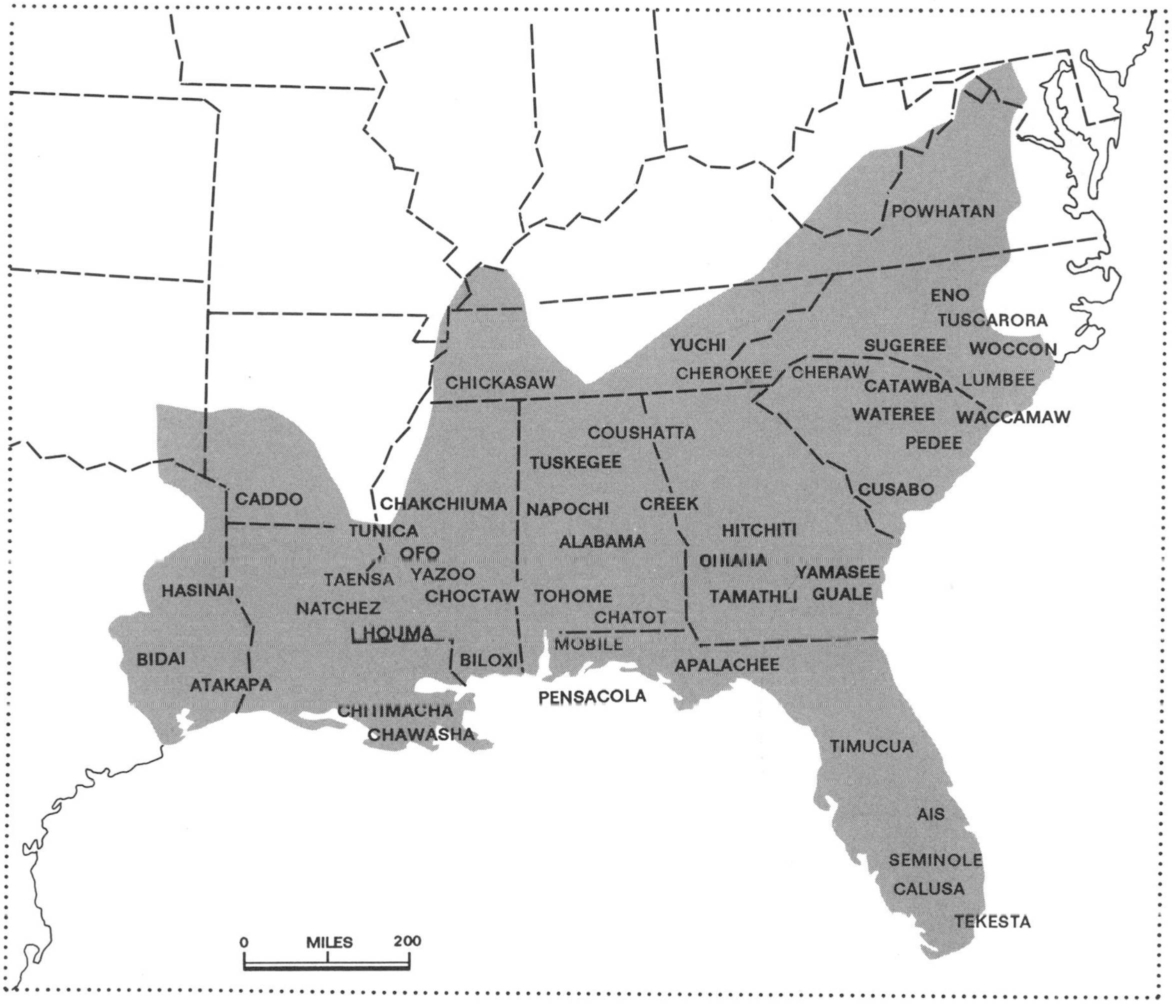
POWHATAN
ENO
TUSCARORA
SUGEREE
WOCCON
YUCHI
CHEROKEE
CHERAW
CATAWBA
LUMBEE
WATEREE
WACCAMAW
PEDEE
CHICKASAW
COUSHATTA
TUSKEGEE
CUSABO
CADDO
CHAKCHIUMA
NAPOCHI
CREEK
TUNICA
HITCHITI
OFO
ALABAMA
TAENSA
YAZOO
YAMASEE
HASINAI
CHOCTAW
TOHOME
TAMATHLI
GUALE
NATCHEZ
CHATOT
HOUMA
MOBILE
BIDAI
BILOXI
APALACHEE
ATAKAPA
PENSACOLA
CHITIMACHA
CHAWASHA
TIMUCUA
AIS
SEMINOLE
CALUSA
TEKESTA
0 MILES 200

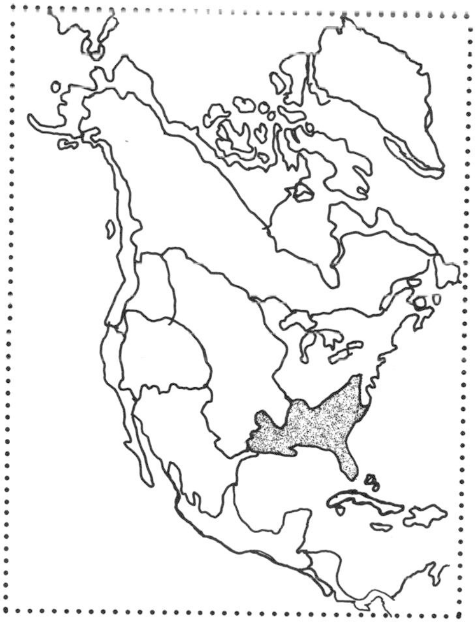

## THE SOUTHEAST CULTURE AREA

North America is divided into different culture areas to aid in the study of historic Native American tribes. Tribes located near the boundaries sometimes overlap with more than one region. In addition, scholars sometimes disagree as to which tribes belong to a particular culture area. The culture areas are determined by the shared customs, life-styles, and languages of the tribal groups.

The approximate traditional tribal boundaries of the Southeast culture area are shown in the larger map, with modern state boundaries. The smaller map shows the culture area in relation to all of North America.

▲ This Cherokee boy and girl, photographed on a North Carolina reservation in 1939, wear costumes heavily influenced by the style of the Plains tribes rather than those of their native Southeast.

# CHAPTER ONE

# ROOTS

People have lived in what is now the United States (as well as Canada, Mexico, and Central and South America) for some 20,000 years, if not longer. Anthropologists believe that Asian hunters crossed to the Western Hemisphere over the land bridge that once stretched across the present-day Bering Strait (between Siberia and Alaska) during the last ice age. The hunters gradually made their way south and east, into the continents of North and South America.

Throughout the many centuries that followed this migration, the descendants of these peoples pushed onward, developing new cultures. Some tribes retained their ancestors' way of life as hunters, while other groups found new ways to survive—as seed gatherers, fishers, villagers, and as farmers. As their diverse cultures spread throughout both American continents, the early Native Americans developed many skills. They became proficient at the cultivation of numerous crops; the arts of pottery, sculpture, beadwork, and metalworking, to name a few; a wealth of languages and ritual practices; and sophisticated techniques in mathematics, architecture, and construction.

Eventually, great agricultural civilizations rose and flourished throughout North and South America, controlled from capital cities featuring mighty temples and many thousands of inhabitants. These cultures included the Inca of present-day Peru, the Maya of what is now Central America, the Aztec of Mexico (which evolved from the earlier Olmec and Toltec) and—in what later became the Southeastern United States—the temple-mound-builders of the Mississippian Culture. The land once chiefly inhabited by the Mississippian people and their descendants stretches eastward from the Mississippi River to the Atlantic seaboard, and south from the Ohio River to the Gulf of Mexico. It encompasses most or all of the present states of Alabama, Florida, Georgia, Louisiana, Mississippi, North Carolina, South Carolina, and Tennessee, parts of what are now Arkansas, Kentucky, Missouri, Virginia, and West Virginia, and the southernmost portions of Illinois, Indiana, and Ohio.

## THE LAND

The Southeastern section of the North American continent was, and in many areas still is, a naturally rich land—rich in sunshine, plant and animal life, and fertile soil. The forests contained a wide variety of game, ranging from squirrel and fox to deer and bear, and all manner of birds. Bison roamed the coastal plains near the Gulf of

▲ Chucalissa Indian Village, situated on a bluff over-looking the Mississippi River near Memphis, Tennessee, flourished as a Mississippian Culture center between A.D. 1100 and 1500. These thatched-roof huts, recon-structed by archaeologists atop original Mississippian earthworks, are part of a complex that also includes cer-emonial mounds and open plazas.

Mexico. The diverse plant life included reeds along the coasts and extensive inland pine forests. When migrating tribes first arrived in the Southeast thcusands of years ago, they shared in this abundance, and these early peoples pros-pered in the area. Later, as they developed meth-ods of farming, the valleys of the region's many rivers and streams became the centers of a new agricultural civilization.

## THE FIRST SOUTHEASTERNERS

Archaeologists have found evidence of human hunters in the Southeast from nearly 10,000 years ago—simple tools, weapons, and a human skeleton discovered in Russell Cave, Alabama, have been dated at approximately 8000 B.C. By then tribal peoples in the Americas had already begun to experiment with the cultivation of crops such as corn. Over the next several thousand years, the peoples of the Southeast

began to develop a more permanent, village-centered culture among the valleys and streams of the Ohio and, later, the Mississippi and other rivers. They still hunted, fished, and gathered wild plants as their ancestors did, but they also cultivated a portion of their food, raising corn, pumpkins, squash, and beans, among other crops.

As their dependence on agriculture in-creased—and their need to move in search of food lessened—the people of these early South-eastern cultures developed skills, arts, and reli-gious practices in some ways very similar to their

▲ The head and tail of a turkey adorn this bowl carved from limestone. It was found at the well-known Moundville site in Alabama.

▲ The people of the Mississippian Culture often carved soft stone into pipe bowls decorated with the figure of an animal or person. This example comes from Kentucky.

distant relatives in present-day Mexico and Central and South America. Each fashioned tools and jewelry from copper, created beautiful pottery from clay, and, most importantly, built a rich religious heritage centered on the power of the sun and the construction of earthen temple and burial mounds.

# THE MISSISSIPPIAN CULTURE

Anthropologists have learned much about these early peoples from the discovery of these ancient mounds and the surrounding villages. Historic artifacts that offer clues to the details of their daily lives have been unearthed at these sites. Two such mound-building cultures that were important to the development of the Southeastern Native Americans are known as the Adena and the Hopewell. Both groups flourished near

the Ohio River and were subsequently named for the present-day locations of the villages. Archaeologists estimate that the Adena Culture thrived between 1000 B.C. and A.D. 700 in what are now southern Ohio, Illinois, and West Virginia; although evidence of Adena villages and mounds as far south as the Gulf Coast of Louisiana suggests that these early cultures were spread extensively by a great trade network, which linked many Southeastern peoples.

The Hopewell Culture also began near the Ohio (about 300 B.C.), but it spread to parts of present-day Louisiana, Alabama, Georgia, and even Florida before it declined around A.D. 600.

The practices and customs of the Adena and Hopewell peoples, both of whom farmed extensively and built great burial mounds without the help of beasts of burden or the wheel, gradually formed the basis of a new culture that would eventually become the most advanced on the North American continent. This new agrarian civilization, which would survive until the Europeans arrived to conquer what they called the New World in the 16th century A.D., has been largely overshadowed in history by the mighty Mexican and Central American cultures that may have influenced it to some extent. But the people of the Mississippian Culture, as it is now known, have left much evidence of a complex civilization rich in ceremony, art, and accomplishment.

Cahokia Mounds in Illinois (just across the Mississippi River from St. Louis, Missouri) is a stunning example of the heights to which the Mississippian people—named for the mighty river on whose banks their culture developed—

rose, reaching a peak several hundred years before the Europeans came. Once the largest Native American city in North America with a population of over 40,000, Cahokia has been unearthed and preserved as a historic site. It contains some 85 temple and burial mounds—including Monks Mound, which at 100 feet in height and 14 acres in width is the largest ancient earthwork in the United States. A great palisade wall once surrounded the city, and at one time the site also featured an astronomical observatory employing wood poles, which has been called "Woodhenge" for its similarity in design and function to England's famous Stonehenge site.

Much has been learned about the Mississippian way of life from Cahokia and other sites like it, such as those at Moundville, Alabama; Etowah, Kolomoki, and Okmulgee, Georgia; Natchez and Winterville, Mississippi; Spiro, Oklahoma; and Chucalissa, Tennessee. These cities revealed that the Mississippian Culture revolved around agriculture and ritual, with temple and burial mounds surrounded by villages and fields of corn (the major crop), beans, pumpkins, and squash. Most cities featured at least one major mound topped by a temple, which contained an "eternal fire" that was kept burning continuously. Burial mounds were usually situated across from the temple-mounds, separated by an open field or plaza where games and ceremonies were held. Historians generally agree that to build as large and complex a city as Cahokia required a large, organized society with a knowledge of mathematics and science, and with a labor force of many thousands working for many years.

In addition to their architectural feats, the Mississippian people became highly skilled in agricultural techniques and such crafts as pottery, metalworking, and weaving. Examples of many kinds of ceramic pottery have been found at the Mississippian Culture sites, ranging from colorful, polished jars to bottles and shallow bowls. Pottery imprinted with fabric designs has been discovered, leading historians to believe that the Mississippians wove fabrics similar to muslin or burlap.

The rich Mississippian Culture thrived throughout the Southeast for centuries, reaching a peak about A.D. 1300. Exactly what brought about the end of the Mississippian mound-builder cultures is not known, but it is believed that these sophisticated, peaceful peoples may have been attacked and conquered by fiercer neighboring tribes, who then adopted a number

▲ Silhouetted against the setting sun in Pinson, Tennessee, is Saul's Mound, built by Indians of the Hopewell or Mississippian Culture nearly 2,000 years ago. At a height of 72 feet, Saul's Mound is the second-tallest Native American mound in the United States.

of Mississippian customs into their own less highly developed cultures. When Europeans first visited the Americas about 200 years later, the Southeastern tribes they met, most notably the Natchez, displayed many of the religious and technological ways of the Mississippians that preceded them. But along with inter-tribal conquest, the coming of the Europeans—and the guns, disease, and greed they brought with them—contributed to the decline of the Mississippian Culture.

## THE MOUND-BUILDERS

Thousands of years ago, tribal groups across the North American continent began to build various styles of earthen mounds to serve a number of different functions. Some of the earliest examples of mounds discovered by archaeologists in the United States were not constructed for any particular purpose but were actually piles of refuse—shells, broken tools, and other artifacts, bones from both animals and humans—that grew over the centuries. The objects that were recovered from these mounds have helped archaeologists determine that humans have lived on this continent for more than 10,000 years, and they have revealed much about the life of those early peoples.

The most enlightening mounds, however, are those that were built for specific purposes—as

monuments to gods or animals, sacred temples, or tombs for the honored dead. Although a number of major mounds—especially effigy mounds, built to resemble animals—can be found scattered throughout the American Midwest, the Southeastern peoples of the Adena, Hopewell, and Mississippian Cultures were the great mound-builders, who constructed temple and burial mounds.

One of the most remarkable things about the Native American mounds is the fact that they were created without the use of beasts of burden or the wheel. Animal-shaped effigy mounds were often constructed by piling countless baskets of earth over a base of stones and clay. A stunning example of this is the Serpent Mound in south-

ern Ohio, a great wall of earth stretching for a quarter-mile in the shape of a giant, striking snake. Although it contains no remains or artifacts and appears to have been built by the Adena people as a monument sometime before A.D. 700, the Serpent Mound is surrounded by several small, cone-shaped burial mounds typical of the Adena style, some of which did contain various objects.

Burial mounds were often constructed with a crypt at the center. The area above the crypt contained objects that may have been possessions of the deceased. Since the Mississippians and their Adena and Hopewell ancestors apparently believed in life after death, the placing of objects in burial mounds "prepared" the dead for the next

# EFFIGY MOUNDS, IOWA

A remarkable group of animal-shaped mounds is found at a site called Effigy Mounds in Iowa. There are nearly 200 mounds at this site, about 30 of which are in the form of bears—which, as shown here, appear to march in formation—and soaring birds. Such effigy mounds were probably built to honor animals considered sacred by the people, and they may have been used as ceremonial grounds or bases of temples. Although a few effigy mounds can be found in the Southeast, most have been discovered west of the Mississippi and are often quite different from Southeastern mounds.

life in much the same way as the entombment of ancient Egyptian kings with their possessions in the pyramids.

The styles of mounds differed among the three major mound-building cultures of the Southeast. The people of the Adena Culture began burying their dead in large circular areas defined by earthen walls. Successive burials created tall, conical mounds—many of which survive today, nearly 3,000 years after their creation. The largest known Adena burial mound, the Grave Creek Mound in present-day Moundsville, West Virginia, is 69 feet tall. Built over 2,000 years ago and preserved today as an historic site, Grave Creek was once encircled by a 40-foot-wide moat and was part of an important Adena religious center.

The second mound-builder civilization was the Hopewell Culture. Hopewell mounds were generally round and were often built in groups and surrounded by walls of earth. Examples of Hopewell mounds can be found today in a wide area stretching from Ohio to the Gulf of Mexico. They range from the impressive Mound City National Monument near Chillicothe, Ohio, to the Marksville site just west of the Mississippi River in Louisiana.

Mound City contains nearly two dozen burial mounds enclosed by a earthwork wall. Bearing names such as Death Mask Mound, Mica Grave Mound, and Mound of the Pipes, these unique mounds are more cone-shaped than other examples from the Hopewell Culture. By contrast, the two Marksville mounds, built in the typically round Hopewell style, are situated on a hilltop that once overlooked a tributary of the Mississippi River.

The mound-building cultures of the Southeast reached their greatest heights with the third group, the Mississippian civilization. A remarkable Mississippian achievement that still survives today as an historic site is the mound city of Cahokia, described elsewhere in this chapter. Other important Mississippian temple-mound cities can be found in Georgia, at the Etowah, Kolomoki, and Okmulgee sites, as well as in Tennessee, Alabama, and Oklahoma. But with its 85 mounds and many other unique features, it is Cahokia—situated in Collinsville, Illinois, di-

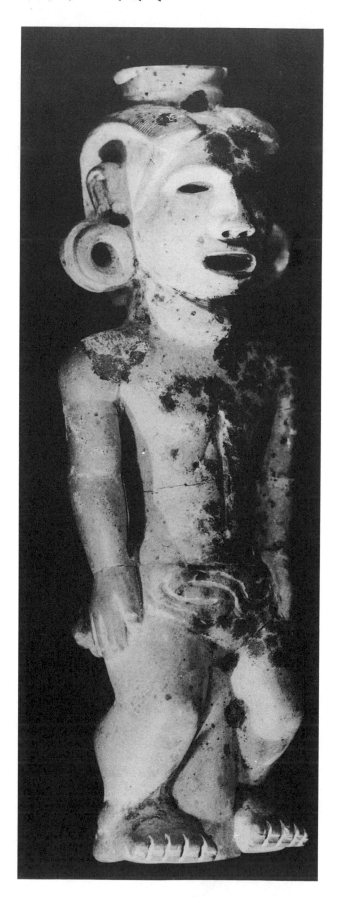

▶ An artisan of the Adena Culture carved this pipe in the shape of a human figure. This artifact was discovered in an Adena burial mound near Chillicothe, Ohio.

▲ An engraving from 1853 shows two young Choctaw men. The man at right wears a nose ring; the face of the man at left is painted. Although both men wear European-style clothing, they wear Choctaw hats.

rectly across the Mississippi from St. Louis—that stands as a tribute to the great feats of the mound-builders of the Southeast.

## THE TRIBES OF THE SOUTHEAST

The Southeastern Native Americans encountered by the European explorers in the 1500s were in many cases the direct descendants of the temple-mound-builders, but they represented only the remnants of tribes who had enjoyed the peak of Mississippian Culture two centuries earlier. As noted previously, historians theorize that the Mississippians themselves had been conquered by and absorbed into more warlike tribes. But for the most part, farming and religion remained the

central parts of the Southeastern culture, and various aspects of the great temple-mound cultures were still in evidence. The Yuchi of Tennessee, the Creek tribes of Alabama and Georgia, the Timucua of Florida, and the Natchez of the lower Mississippi Valley most directly resembled the Mississippian mound-builders.

As Native American tribes (also known as nations) migrated into the Southeast as individual groups, many of them settled into their own territories to coexist within larger nations called confederacies. The Creek were an example of a great Southeastern confederacy, made up of many smaller tribes with common origins—including the Tuskegee, Alabama, Coosa, Hitchiti, Okmulgee, and Seminole peoples—who spread throughout present-day Georgia and Alabama (and, in the case of the Seminole, into Florida).

These nations and confederacies developed over the centuries, as the once-mobile Southeasterners adapted their life-styles to the areas that would eventually become their traditional homelands. Their life-styles generally fell into two cat-

# THE SEMINOLE

Around the beginning of the 19th century, a Southeastern nation belonging to the Creek Confederacy of Alabama and Georgia broke away and moved to the south, settling in Florida under the name of Seminole (Creek for "runaway"). Throughout the rest of the century, as other native Southeasterners were forcibly removed from their ancestral lands by the U.S. government, the Seminole people fought to stay in their newly adopted home in the Everglades. Although many Seminole were removed and resettled west of the Mississippi, groups of them continued to fight U.S. troops for decades. As a result, a substantial Seminole population remains in Florida to this day. This photo, taken in Miami in 1926, shows a Seminole family posing in front of their thatched-roof dwellings, dressed in the tribe's traditional festive garb.

egories—that of those who lived in coastal areas, and that of the inland peoples (including mountain dwellers). Naturally, coastal tribes, such as the Ais along the Atlantic and the Atakapa and Pensacola on the Gulf of Mexico, were largely dependent on the sea for their way of life. But the inland groups—who had easy access to rivers and freshwater streams, fertile land for farming and woodlands teeming with edible plants and game—could hunt, fish, and raise crops, and lived a rich and varied life amid the abundance of nature.

Geographically, the inland tribes dominated the Southeast. Four of what would later become known as "The Five Civilized Tribes"—the Choctaw, Chickasaw, Cherokee, and Creek Nations—lived among the fertile fields stretching from the Mississippi to the Atlantic Coast, and all farmed extensively. The Choctaw settled in what is now central Mississippi, while the

# THE LANGUAGES OF THE SOUTHEAST

Many different languages were spoken by the nations of the Southeast. The most widespread was Muskogean, which was spoken by the Creek and Seminole, among others. The Cherokee, however, spoke their own language, which was similar to the Iroquoian languages spoken by many tribes in the Northeast.

| ALGONQUIAN FAMILY | CADDOAN FAMILY | IROQUOIAN FAMILY |
|---|---|---|
| Lumbee | Caddo | Cherokee |
| Powhatan | | Tuscarora |

| MUSKOGEAN FAMILY | | |
|---|---|---|
| Alabama | | |
| Apalachee | NATCHEZ | SIOUAN FAMILY |
| Calusa | Natchez | Catawba |
| Chickasaw | | Yuchi |
| Choctaw | | |
| Coushatta | | |
| Creek | TIMUCUAN | TUNICAN |
| Seminole | Timucua | Tunica |
| Yamasee | | Yazoo |

Chickasaw lived to the north of them in northern Mississippi and western Tennessee and Kentucky. The Creek Confederacy was spread throughout Alabama and Georgia, while their bitter traditional enemies, the Cherokee, dominated the areas to the north, in eastern Tennessee, northern Georgia, and the western Carolinas. The Tuscarora claimed most of North Carolina, while the Powhatan Confederacy occupied much of what is now Virginia. The Timucua thrived in southern Georgia and the northern half of the Florida peninsula. And the fifth of the "Civilized Tribes"—the Seminole—were a branch of the Creek Confederacy who moved south in the early 1800s to settle in central and southern Florida, where some of them still reside today among the Everglades.

## MANY NATIONS, MANY LANGUAGES

Virtually every aspect of Native American culture—dress, diet, religious practices, forms of transportation and shelter, ways of raising and gathering food, arts and crafts, music and dance, and especially language—differs in varying degrees from nation to nation (nations can also be referred to as tribes). Native American languages, in fact, are so numerous that they are difficult to classify. There have been an estimated 1,200 or so native languages in use in the Americas at one time or another. The several hundred North American languages have been classified into some 50 families and six "superfamilies." A few of these families are the basis for most of the languages spoken by the peoples of the Southeast.

The most widespread language family was Muskogean, which was seldom spoken in other parts of the continent and has been referred to as "the language of the Southeast." The dialects of such dominant Southeastern nations as the Choctaw, Chickasaw, Creek, Seminole, and others, were all derived from Muskogean. Other languages (such as those in the Algonquian or Siouan families) were heard more often in other regions, and the Southeastern nations that spoke them may have been descendants of tribal peoples who had broken off from their main groups and migrated to the Southeast centuries before.

Still, traditionally non-Southeastern languages were spoken by a great many of the Southeastern tribes. The populous Cherokee na-

▲ Chief Pleasant Porter (1840–1907), a Creek leader and educator, in a photo taken around 1900.

tion, for example, spoke a language derived from the Iroquoian family, which dominated much of what is now the Northeastern United States. Another Northeastern language family, the Algonquian, was the basis for the language of such Virginia-area tribes as the Powhatan. (Some scholars feel that Powhatan and the Tuscarora of North Carolina are the southernmost part of the Northeast culture region, but they are often included with the Indians of the Southeast because they shared many of their ways of life.) A version of the Siouan tongue spoken by the tribes of the Great Plains was used by the Catawba and the Yuchi. And groups scattered throughout the Southeast also spoke languages based on other families as well.

# LIVING ON THE LAND

\* \* \* \* \* \* \* \* \* \* \* \*

## SOUTHEASTERN BEAUTY

▼ Numerous lakes and swampy areas rich in fish and wildlife are found throughout Florida. The region was home to the Seminole, Timucua, and Apalachee.

\* \* \* \* \* \* \* \* \* \* \* \* \*

◁   The extensive hardwood forests of the Southeast provided the Native Americans there with abundant deer and other game.

▷   The Great Smoky Mountains run through modern-day North Carolina and Tennessee. This region is the ancestral homeland of the Cherokee. At 6,642 feet, Clingmans Dome (shown here) is the highest point in the range.

▽   The marshy Everglades of Florida cover about 5,000 square miles. Today, much of the region is part of Everglades National Park; four Seminole reservations are also in the Everglades.

# ANIMALS OF IMPORTANCE

✱ ✱ ✱ ✱ ✱ ✱ ✱ ✱ ✱ ✱ ✱ ✱ ✱

▶ The magnificent bald eagle, once common throughout the Southeast, is today an endangered species. Thanks to federal protection and increased environmental awareness, bald eagles are making a comeback in Florida.

◀ Alligators were an important source of food and skins for many Native Americans in the Southeast. Here an alligator rests on a fallen cypress tree in southern Florida.

▼ Deer were an important and abundant food source for the Native Americans of the Southeast.

✱ ✱ ✱ ✱ ✱ ✱ ✱ ✱ ✱ ✱ ✱ ✱ ✱

# THE MOUND-BUILDERS

✱ ✱ ✱ ✱ ✱ ✱ ✱ ✱ ✱ ✱ ✱ ✱ ✱

◀ Craftspeople from all the mound-building cultures often used human or animal figures, or effigies, to decorate objects. In this example, a frog is part of a pottery vessel.

▼ Monks Mound at Cahokia, a Mississippian Culture temple-mound city in present-day Illinois, was built in 14 stages between A.D. 900 and 1150 and was once topped by a massive temple. Towering at a height of 100 feet and covering some 14 acres, Monks Mound is the largest prehistoric earthwork in the United States.

✱ ✱ ✱ ✱ ✱ ✱ ✱ ✱ ✱ ✱ ✱ ✱ ✱

The craftspeople of the Hopewell Culture often fashioned adornments and implements in the shape of animals and birds. This copper effigy of a peregrine falcon was found in a burial mound at Mound City National Monument near Chillicothe, Ohio.

A Mississippian temple-mound dominates the landscape at Mound State Park in Moundville, Alabama. A reconstructed temple sits atop the earthwork.

* * * * * * * * * * * * *

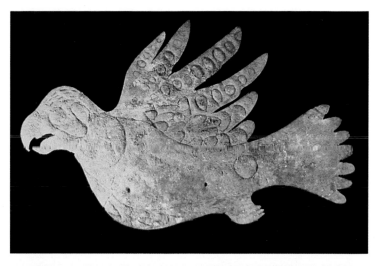

▲ The Cherokee woman in this contemporary photo pounds meal using a wooden staff and a hollowed-out tree stump as mortar and pestle.

# CHAPTER TWO

\* \* \* \* \* \* \* \* \* \* \* \* \*

# LIVING

he great abundance of fish, game, and gathered or cultivated crops allowed most Southeastern tribes to live fairly comfortable lives before and for a century or so after the Europeans came to North America. The people worked hard to provide their families with food, clothing, and shelter; fought fiercely to protect themselves from their enemies; thanked and worshiped their maker with rituals and ceremonies; skillfully created original arts and crafts; enjoyed singing and ceremonial dancing; and took part in a variety of ceremonial games and sports.

## THE GREATEST ABUNDANCE

When Europeans first visited the tribal peoples of what is now the Southeastern United States, they were amazed at the rich variety of foods eaten by their native hosts. The numerous crops raised by the Southeasterners, combined with the many wild plants they gathered, the various animals they hunted, and the fish and other creatures they obtained from nearby waters, resulted in a great abundance of foods.

As in any civilization, the availability of food was central to the cultures of the Southeastern Native Americans. The earliest Southeasterners

followed their food sources, and trapped, caught, or otherwise gathered their food from their surroundings. Mountain and forest dwellers such as the Cherokee and the Creek hunted for game and gathered berries and other wild plants. Those peoples residing near rivers or the coasts—ranging from the Natchez of the Mississippi valley and the Calusa of Florida to the Powhatan of Virginia's Atlantic coast—also harvested the fish and other marine life of nearby waters.

Unlike the Native American peoples of other areas of North America, the Southeasterners—especially those along rivers and streams—generally lived on extremely fertile land with an abundant supply of fresh water. Their early efforts to raise crops were successful, and over the centuries the Southeastern peoples developed a culture that depended chiefly on farming for its survival.

## FARMING AND GATHERING

The most important crop to the Southeasterners—indeed, to most cultures throughout the Americas—was corn. Corn was first cultivated by Native Americans. It grew well in many parts of the Americas, could be stored throughout the winter, and prepared in a great variety of ways. Other crops raised by the Southeasterners in-

# AGRICULTURE

This detail from a 1564 engraving by French artist/explorer Jacques Le Moyne shows Timucua in Florida preparing the soil and planting seeds. Although Le Moyne's journal describes a hoe made of bone with wooden handles, the artist actually depicted the Indians using a European hoe or mattock. The Native Americans of the Southeast were very sophisticated farmers who grew many varieties of corn and other crops. The Creek could prepare corn in 40 different ways.

Jacques Le Moyne was among the first European explorers to document his impressions of Native Americans in both words and pictures. His many illustrations and descriptions provide nearly all available information on the life of the Timucua, since the tribe was virtually wiped out by the early 19th century.

cluded pumpkins, squash, potatoes, sweet potatoes, several varieties of beans, peas, cabbages, melons, and even mushrooms. The vegetables and fruits that these crops yielded were prepared in many ways. They were sometimes cooked by themselves to supplement corn, meat, or fish; just as often, they were blended in recipes with corn, other staples, or plants gathered from the wild. Throughout the Southeastern region, farming was the central activity of many tribes, and a village's entire population would often take part in the efforts.

Using hoes fashioned from wood, stone, or bone, the community readied the land for each season's crops. The ground was prepared and the seed planted in the spring by both the men and the women of the tribe, but during much of the summer growing season most of the work was done by the women. At harvest time the men joined in again and helped the women cut the crops with scythes (long-handled knives with thin, crescent-shaped wooden blades), gather them in woven baskets, and store much of the harvest in community storehouses, called granaries, for the winter. Each year's harvest was celebrated by many Southeastern nations with an elaborate religious ritual known as the Green Corn Ceremony, which marked the start of a new season of plenty with worship, dancing, feasting, and merrymaking.

About 60 percent of the Southeasterners' food supply came from plant sources that were either cultivated in the tribal fields or gathered in the wild. All manner of fruits, herbs, vegetables, and spices were picked in the wild and put to interesting and varied use in countless recipes. Among the most popular wild plants gathered in the Southeast were wild and scuppernong grapes, strawberries, huckleberries, crabapples, wild rice, peanuts, hickory nuts, sweet potatoes,

# HUNTING TECHNIQUES

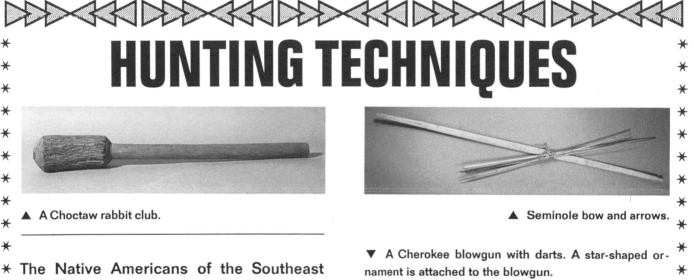

▲ A Choctaw rabbit club.

▲ Seminole bow and arrows.

▼ A Cherokee blowgun with darts. A star-shaped ornament is attached to the blowgun.

The Native Americans of the Southeast were primarily farmers, but hunting was also an important source of food. Bows and arrows were used to hunt larger game such as deer. Smaller animals such as rabbits were caught in traps or snares and then killed with a club. A hunting method used in the Southeast was the blowgun. Usually made from a hollow length of cane or reed, the blowgun fired darts—sometimes with poisoned tips—propelled by the hunter's breath.

and various other roots and tubers, syrup from maple trees (from which maple sugar was made) and persimmons—which the Tunica and the Natchez used to make a variety of breads. Southeastern recipes were frequently spiced with wild cinnamon, sassafras, salt, and seeds from the sunflower, palmetto, and pond lily. These spices were frequently combined with oil—such as that boiled out of bear fat—and the resulting blend was stored for the winter in jars.

## HUNTING AND FISHING

The Native Southeasterners hunted and fished for the remaining 40 percent of their diet. Although farming was their chief occupation, many Indians of the region were also skilled hunters, trappers, and fishers. The spear and the bow and arrow—with points made of flint, bone, or, later, metal—were the most common weapons of the hunt. Snare traps constructed from sticks, twine, and saplings were also used, as were knives and,

▲ Although farming was their primary occupation, Southeastern Indians were also skilled hunters. This engraving from 1564 portrays an ingenious method used by the Timucua of Florida to hunt deer. Draped in deerskins, with bows and arrows at the ready, the hunters stealthily prepare to attack their unsuspecting prey.

as among the Choctaw and Cherokee, even blowguns and darts.

Deer and bear were the primary large game animals, and some tribes, especially the Natchez of Louisiana, hunted bison before the introduction of the rifle in the 17th century, which brought their extermination in that area of the country. But many smaller animals, such as rabbits, raccoons, opossums, squirrels, and birds, including passenger pigeons, wild turkeys, and quail, also supplied meat.

Meat—whether it came from game, fish, or fowl—was prepared any number of ways. Stewing in earthen pots with vegetables and spices or

▲ Fishing was an important means of gathering food to many peoples of the Southeast, especially those living along rivers or on the Atlantic or Gulf coasts. This 1585 engraving depicts a group who inhabited what is now North Carolina fishing with spears, traps, and nets.

grilling over an open fire were among the most popular methods of cooking, although food was also dried and smoked.

Tribes living along the rivers and the coastlines depended greatly on the waters for much of their food, especially since coastal land was harder to farm than that found farther inland. The flesh of such aquatic animals as otters, beavers, manatees (sea cows), turtles, shellfish, alligators, and countless species of fish supplemented the diets of these tribes. The Indians fished with hooks, traps, nets, dams, arrows, spears, and even with their bare hands. Perhaps the most unusual fishing method among the Southeasterners, however, was the practice of spreading roots and herbs over the water to drug the fish, which were much easier to catch in a stunned state.

As did nearly all Native American cultures, the peoples of the Southeast used the hides and fur of the animals they hunted as a source of clothing or ornament, constructed implements from the bones, and cord from sinew. They wasted nothing. The tusks and hide of the manatee, for example, were used to make tools, jewelry, and leather. Turtles were sought not only for food, but also for their shells and eggs. Even alligators—which were often speared or wrestled into submission by particularly daring hunters— were prized as much for their distinctive skins as for their meat.

▲ Three Seminole girls in traditional rickrack apparel stand in a dugout canoe in the swampy Everglades of Florida. This photo dates to 1907.

## MAIZE: THE STAFF OF LIFE

Nearly every Native American culture that raised much of its own food depended heavily on one major crop for its prosperity: corn, or "maize," by its proper name. Many people don't realize that corn is a Native American food plant—actually a grass, like rice, wheat, and other grains—that was unknown in Europe until explorers brought it back with them from their voyages in the 15th and 16th centuries. First developed in South America, the cultivation of maize began as early as 5,000 years ago and spread throughout North America. The crop eventually became the main-stay of tribes in many regions of the continent, especially in the Southeast.

Every agrarian nation of the Southeast raised corn, and some tribes made it the center of their spiritual as well as physical lives. Many Native American cultures attributed a host of spiritual powers to the plant, believing it to be a gift of the spirits, and stories abound about the sacred origins of maize and the deities responsible for an abundant harvest. The Creek peoples, for example, have traditionally celebrated the coming of each summer's new crop of corn with an eight-day series of festivities known as Green Corn, or "busk" ceremonies. A central part of the religion of the Creek and other Southeastern nations, the Green Corn Ceremony was—and still is—a high point of every year for the tribe, commemorating the sacred gift of corn.

Corn was used by the Southeastern Indians in an amazing variety of ways. The Creek were reported to have had more than 40 different ways

▲ Southeasterners hunted with a variety of weapons, including spears, bows and arrows, traps, and even blowguns. The Cherokee and Choctaw were very proficient with blowguns, such as the one being loaded here by Wood Bell, a Choctaw guide at the reconstructed Chucalissa Indian Village in Memphis, Tennessee.

▲ Corn was a staple food for the Native Americans of the Southeast. In this photograph from 1907, a Seminole man uses a wooden pestle and a hollow log to pound dried corn kernels into meal.

to prepare corn dishes. They—along with the Chickasaw, Seminole, and most other Southeastern tribes—roasted corn directly over a fire or hot coals, stewed it, boiled it, blended it with all sorts of meats and vegetables and ground it into meal (which was used in a number of beverages and other types of foods, as well as for baking bread). Also, corn's ability to be stored in granaries over long periods of time made it available for use during any season. Because of corn's great contribution to the quality of their lives over the centuries, the Southeasterners held it in high esteem. And due to the work of the Native American farmers who cultivated it over the centuries, American society still enjoys the benefits of this extremely versatile food source today.

## VILLAGE LIFE AND GOVERNMENT

Many Southeastern tribes were organized into villages or towns in much the same way as the Mississippian Culture's life revolved around cities or major population centers in the period prior to A.D. 1300. Although the Natchez culture, in particular, most closely resembled that of the earlier Mississippian mound-builders, the Creek, Choctaw, Seminole, Cherokee, and Chickasaw also centered their existence around villages that contained both individual dwellings and public places.

The villages or towns of these tribes consisted of strings of dwellings usually made of reeds and bark. The dwellings were often built along streams or in clearings near the planting fields and were connected by trails that wound through the countryside. Cherokee villages (along with those of other Southeastern tribes) had a center or square with a council house, where ceremonies, festivals, and other public occasions were held. Among the Creek, Choctaw, and others, larger towns containing several hundred dwellings often featured palisade walls and moats for defense and served as centers for smaller surrounding villages.

Such villages were the center of Southeastern community life. Here the people worked together to plant the corn and other crops during the

# SOUTHEASTERN VILLAGES

The Indian village of Pomeioc in what is now North Carolina, in a 1585 rendering by the English artist John White. Although Pomeioc was most likely a Tuscarora town with Algonquian features, it represented a village design common to many Southeastern nations at the time of the first contact with Europeans. This layout featured a number of thatched-roof dwellings made of reed and bark, long open structures that served as meeting or council houses or as grain storage areas, and an open central plaza for ceremonies and games. The entire village was surrounded by a wooden palisade or fence.

▲ A European view of an Indian village in Virginia in the
mid-1500s. The importance of agriculture to the peoples
of the Southeast is seen by the fields growing different
crops. A ceremonial dance is shown at bottom right.

▲ A group of Seminole in traditional dress stand by their chickees in a village near Miami, Florida, in 1931. The palm trees in the background provide the material for the thatched roofs of the chickees.

spring, harvest them in autumn, and store them in public granaries, so that everyone would have enough to eat during the winter. It was in the village square, with its council house or ceremonial ground, that the people would gather to share both solemn and joyous rituals such as the Green Corn Ceremony. Towns and villages also figured prominently in the Southeastern Indians' government and relations between peoples. War parties were organized in villages, and warfare was generally conducted by raiding the villages of enemy tribes. Among the Choctaw, Chickasaw, and other tribes, rival towns would often oppose each other, not only in war, but in ball games or other athletic contests.

The towns of the Creek nation had an interesting role in the conduct of government, war, and peace. Actually a confederacy of smaller tribes rather than a single, united people, the Creek (or Muskogean) nation was divided into two types of towns, the "White" and "Red," or the "Peace" and "War" towns. The White towns played a pivotal role in peaceful governmental affairs, controlled such important ceremonies as the Green Corn festival, and chose the principal chief of the confederacy from among their leaders. The Red towns, by contrast, took the lead in warfare against tribal enemies (or occasionally against each other) and supplied the confederacy with its Great Warrior, or battle chief.

## THE FAMILY AND THE CLAN

Much of Southeastern Native American life revolved around marriage and the family. The customs and traditions of the family, in turn, were dominated by the ancient laws of the *clan*. A clan was a kind of extended family within a Southeastern tribe. Clan membership was passed on through the mother, in what is called *matrilineal descent*. Clans were often named for animals (such as the Panther clan of the Creek). Members of clans enjoyed various rights and

privileges, such as a share in clan property or the exclusive right to special titles, songs, chants, and deities (or spirits).

The clan laws were of great importance to the Southeastern Indians and were highly respected. The customs of marriage, for example, were dictated by the clan laws. Marriage within one's clan was strictly forbidden and prior to the mid-1800s could have been punishable by death. A person's father always belonged to a different clan than his or her mother. And since the line of descent was matrilineal, a child automatically became a member of his or her mother's clan.

In some Southeastern tribes, a man and woman would marry simply by agreeing to do so and exchanging gifts between their families. The village or tribe would celebrate the union with feasting and dancing. Usually, the newly married couple would then set up a household in a dwelling of their own. It was not uncommon, however, for newlyweds to move into the dwelling of one or the other's parents, creating an extended family.

The institution of marriage was taken very seriously throughout the region. Divorce was not uncommon, but it was often a last resort after marital trouble. Among the Cherokee, for instance, divorce would only occur after intervention by the couple's mothers had failed to patch things up. A Cherokee woman—who by law and custom owned her family's house and property—would often start a divorce by literally throwing her husband's belongings out of their dwelling.

Infidelity was a serious offense; married people who committed adultery were reproached by the entire community, and they were frequently banished from their village. In some tribes, however, men were allowed to have more than one wife. A Chickasaw man, for example, could have as many wives as he could support. But this "privilege" did not often extend to Southeastern Indian women, who were usually expected to remain faithful to one husband.

## THE STYLE OF SOUTHEASTERN LIFE

Since men, women, and children alike worked and played in the frequently oppressive heat of the Southeast, they seldom wore many articles of clothing. In summer, especially in Florida and the Gulf Coast, men usually wore only a breechcloth (a simple garment worn around the waist and pelvic area), while in cooler weather they

▲ In this engraving dating from 1590, a Native American in Virginia is shown wearing a breechcloth with an animal tail attached. He carries a bow, an arrow, and a quiver for holding extra arrows.

might add a pair of leggings made of animal hide. Women, too, wore very little during the warmer months in this area—perhaps a skirt woven from coarse cloth or a scarf fashioned from palm fronds and draped over the body. Tribes in the northern section of the region, of course, dressed more warmly, often wearing clothes of hide, fur, cloth, or—after they were introduced by Europeans—cotton or wool. Many Southeasterners later adapted the European materials to fit their own individual tribal styles.

Grooming and personal ornament was important to the native Southeasterners. Men's bodies were often tattooed, or "scratched," as part of a rite of manhood and to signify prowess as a warrior. They adorned themselves with necklaces or pendants of shell or bone. In most tribes, men's

▲ A young Seminole woman wears traditional clothing and jewelry in this photo from around 1907. Her hair is worn in the traditional and elaborate topknot style.

hair was usually kept short; frequently it was shaved, cropped to a roach (a single area of hair in the center of the head), or plucked out in a pattern. The men of such tribes as the Timucua and Pensacola of Florida and the Choctaw of Mississippi, on the other hand, wore their hair long.

Some Southeastern men wore simple feather headdresses, while great warriors, chiefs, or elders sported more elaborate ones, often made from an entire bird or other small animal. Among some tribes, the scalp lock—a section of longer hair left as a challenge to enemies to try to collect the wearer's scalp—was kept whether the rest of the hair was long or short. This custom was more common after contact with Europeans, who spread the primarily northern practice of scalping throughout other parts of North America.

Women of the Southeastern tribes usually wore their hair long. They used combs made of wood, bone, shell, or copper to groom their long

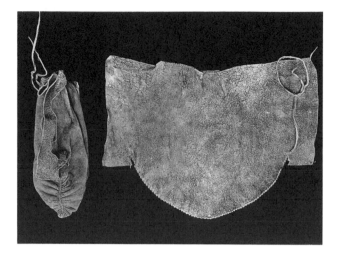

▲ The technique for making a moccasin is shown in this photo. At right is a single piece of buckskin cut to shape. At left is the finished moccasin. This example was made by a Cherokee in North Carolina in 1918.

hair, often braiding it and dressing it with headbands of shells, flowers, or beads. Later, European influence showed in Southeastern women's hairstyles, especially among Florida's Seminole, whose women adopted pompadours. They also had unique styles of their own, such as a Seminole coiffure in which the hair was drawn up from the neck to the forehead, then tied and spread over a frame.

## CHORES AND CRAFTS

From an early age, all members of the Southeastern family worked hard to help their family and tribe prosper. Support of the family and home was the first priority, but most individuals also contributed to the welfare of the tribal village. They took part in such community efforts as harvesting and storing crops for the winter, building council houses, holding public gatherings and ceremonies, and preparing for and waging war. Southeastern men served as, among other things, warriors, hunters, builders, craftsmen, and farmers. Joined in many instances by the boys of the tribe, men felled trees, cleared and tilled the fields, hunted and fished, built the homes and village structures, took part in war parties against tribal enemies, and crafted a wide variety of objects: canoes, tools and weapons, moccasins,

▲ In this 1941 photograph, two Seminole women are making syrup from sugarcane at the Seminole Indian Agency in Florida.

drums, pipes, and household implements. Some specialized in certain skills and worked mainly as farmers, traders, warriors, or fishers. Men also performed important tribal functions as priests, medicine men, and chiefs.

The work done by Native Southeastern women was equally instrumental to the prosperity of both their families and their tribes. They cared for their children and their homes, but women also did a large share of the farming—planting, tending, and harvesting the crops with the help of the children and, sometimes, the men. Using a mortar and pestle (a bowl and grinding implement made of stone, bone, or wood), women and their daughters ground corn into meal for the hundreds of dishes made from it. They prepared, cooked, and preserved what they and their husbands provided for the family's table, wove fabric, and tanned hides to create clothing and blankets.

The women of the Southeast also practiced and passed on to their daughters some of the most beautiful Native American arts. Women and girls of the Cherokee of northern Georgia and the Chitimacha of Louisiana fashioned some of the finest cane basketry ever produced. Weaving strips of cane dyed in a variety of colors into complex geometric patterns, these women made baskets of all shapes and sizes. Along with the Catawba of South Carolina, the Cherokee also became known for creating beautiful, intricate clay pottery.

Southeastern women gathered berries, nuts, acorns, and other wild foodstuffs, not to mention firewood, fresh water, and nearly everything else

# CHICKEES

Designed for comfort in the swampy heat of the Gulf Coast and Florida Everglades, the Seminole chickee was actually a house on stilts. The chickee was built from palmetto or cane on a raised platform that kept its inhabitants safe from snakes and other swamp creatures. The chickee had no walls. Some chickees featured individual canopies, which were rolled up and stored when not needed. This chickee, still used today by Miccosukee Seminole as part of an exhibit of Seminole life, is part of the Shark Valley Indian Village at Everglades National Park in Florida.

their families needed to live besides meat. Their children helped in most of these tasks. The efforts of the entire family contributed to the well-being of the household.

## THE SOUTHEASTERN HOME

The homes of the Southeasterners were sturdily constructed from a number of materials—wood, thatch, bark, and reeds such as cane—in a variety of styles, depending on the area, its climate, and its terrain. The hutlike dwelling used by most Southeastern tribes was simple, functional, and well-suited to its location. It usually featured a raised shelf or scaffold, often made of cane, which functioned as a sleeping area. In the northernmost parts of the region, the people built walled huts designed to keep out the chill of the mountains and the winter season.

Some tribes in the central area of the Southeast actually had two homes for each family, one for winter and one for summer. The winter home was insulated with a clay compound to keep in the warmth generated by an indoor fire or—as among the Choctaw of Mississippi—a kind of sauna using water and heated stones. In contrast, the summer home had its kitchen and oven separated from the sleeping quarters.

Farther south, in such consistently warm ar-

▲ Homes of the Southeastern peoples varied from nation to nation in style as well as materials. The Creek house in this engraving from 1791 is essentially a log cabin with a roof made of reeds. Other Southeasterners lived in huts fashioned entirely from reeds and bark.

eas as Florida and the Gulf Coast, some types of dwellings—such as the Seminole *chickee*—had no walls at all. The chickee was built on stilts to keep its inhabitants safe from snakes, ground moisture, and other discomforts; to protect themselves from insects, the family members also had individual canopies that could be rolled up and stored in the chickee's rafters. In coastal areas, the chickee or other dwellings were usually constructed with timber from the plentiful palmetto tree; inland, cane was the preferred building material.

Whether raising their children, tending their crops, building their homes, or creating unique and beautiful objects, the Native Americans of the Southeast went about their tasks with great skill and conviction and took pride in their work. But the ancient traditions that the Southeasterners followed in pursuing these and other activities—including war, worship, and games—were soon to be seriously threatened by the arrival of the Europeans.

# DAILY LIVING

\* \* \* \* \* \* \* \* \* \* \* \*

## DWELLINGS

▶ The last remnants of Mississippian Culture were represented by the Natchez people, who inhabited the lower Mississippi Valley in present-day Mississippi and Louisiana. This reconstructed earth and thatch dwelling stands today at the Grand Village of the Natchez Indians, a national historic landmark located in Natchez, Mississippi.

▼ A view of thatched-roof huts and a temple-mound (in the background at right) at Chucalissa Indian Village in Tennessee, a reconstructed Mississippian Culture site near Memphis.

\* \* \* \* \* \* \* \* \* \* \* \*

# EVERYDAY ARTISTRY

◀ The cane, or reeds, that grow in the swampy parts of the Southeast were often used for making baskets by the Native Americans. This outstanding example was made by a member of the Alabama tribe living in Texas.

▶ This pottery jar and cover were made by a Cherokee in North Carolina. The decoration on the surface was made by the traditional method of pressing a wooden paddle with the pattern carved on it against the wet clay.

▼ Cherokee women practice the craft of finger-weaving. The colorful sashes made in this way use traditional designs.

✳ ✳ ✳ ✳ ✳ ✳ ✳ ✳ ✳ ✳ ✳ ✳ ✳

# CLOTHING

\* \* \* \* \* \* \* \* \* \* \* \* \*

▲ The Caddo lived in what is today Texas and Oklahoma. They had much in common with the Native Americans of the Plains. These leather leggings with beautiful beaded decoration were meant to protect the legs of a rider on horseback.

▲ After contact with European traders brought brightly colored cloth and other manufactured items to them, the Seminole developed a distinctive turban-style headdress.

▲ The Seminole developed an unusual and beautiful style of clothing made from brightly colored pieces of cloth carefully sewn into elaborate patterns. This example, made in the "big shirt" style, was worn by a man.

▲ This deerskin coat was worn by a Seminole. The cuffs are decorated with beadwork.

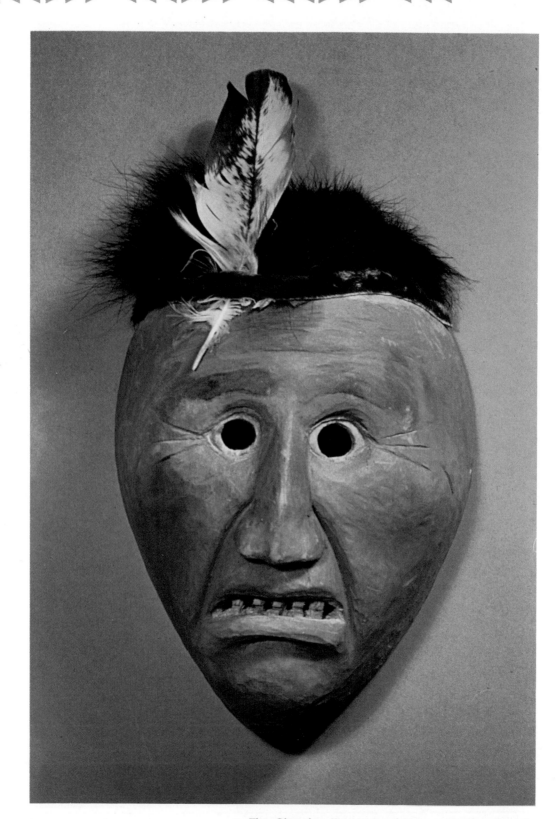

▲ This Cherokee Booger mask represents an evil spirit. It is carved from wood, painted, and decorated with animal fur and a feather.

## CHAPTER THREE

# RITUAL, RELIGION, AND TRADITIONS

he native peoples of the Southeast lived in harmony with their natural surroundings (if not always with each other) for hundreds, and perhaps thousands, of years. Enjoying a great abundance of natural resources and a rich culture, they lived full lives, following customs of work, play, war, and worship that had been passed down through the generations. Through the years between the middle of the 16th and 19th centuries—a period when European contact, exploration, and colonization would eventually threaten their way of life and drive them from their homelands—the Southeastern Indians held on to these traditions. Many of these customs survive today, as do the tribes who practiced them throughout the centuries.

## CREATION STORIES

People of the Southeastern nations told their first European visitors the stories of their tribal origins, several of which involved the entire people's descent from the sun. The Yuchi called themselves "Children of the Sun," and they regarded the sun as the sacred source of all life. Other tribes kept an eternal flame, representing the sun's power on earth, burning in their tem-

ples—in keeping with the traditions of their Mississippian ancestors. The Natchez referred to their tribal leader as "the Great Sun" and forbade any disrespect to the sun. The Yuchi's firm belief that they were descended from the sun made them welcome among the Creek, who also looked on the sun as their father.

Other Southeastern tribal stories recounted the long journeys of their ancestors from distant lands. One story of the Iroquoian-speaking Cherokee nation describes a long and difficult journey from "the Northwest" that ancient Cherokee people made with Algonquian-speaking Lenape and other Northern tribes. The story tells how the tribal groups separated near a large body of water; some (probably the Iroquois) returned to the North, while the Cherokee continued, finally settling in the areas of eastern Tennessee and the Carolinas.

In telling of the ancient bonds that often existed between tribes—however distant their lands may have been—the Cherokee referred to the Lenape as "grandfathers" of all Native Americans of the region. They also called themselves "brothers" of the Iroquois and the Tuscarora (who shared their own Iroquoian language), and "uncles" of such Muskogean-speaking tribes as the Creek, Chickasaw, and Choctaw.

# LEGENDS

## THE CHEROKEE STORY OF LITTLE DEER

Long, long ago the Cherokee people lived in peace with the animals. They hunted only when they needed food or skins for clothing. But then the people learned to make bows and arrows. They began to hunt all the time, even when they didn't need food or clothing.

The deer held a council to discuss the problem. Little Deer was their leader. He spoke wisely, saying, "The people must hunt us to live, but they should respect us and hunt only when they must. I will tell the hunters that they must prepare themselves spiritually for the hunt. They must ask permission before killing one of us. After they kill a deer they must respect its spirit and ask for pardon. If they do not, I will find them and cripple them!"

To this day, when a Cherokee hunter kills a deer, Little Deer runs to the spot and asks the spirit of the deer if it heard the hunter ask for pardon. If the deer says yes, Little Deer departs. But if the deer says no, or if the hunter has killed for no reason, Little Deer finds the hunter and punishes him. For this reason, the Cherokee people respect and thank the deer and all the other animals they hunt.

## STEALING THE SUN: A CREEK STORY

When the world began, there was no sun, and no one could see anything. Fox said that the people on the other side of the earth had light from the sun, but they were too greedy to share it. One day when the people on the other side of the earth weren't looking, Fox tried to grab a piece of the sun in his mouth. But the sun was hot and it burned his mouth. Ever since, Fox has had a black mouth. Opossum decided to steal some light from the sun, hide it in his bushy tail, and bring it back. He sneaked over to the other side of the earth, stole a tiny piece of the sun, and put it into his tail. But the sun was hot and it burned off all the fur on his tail. Ever since, Opossum has had a bald tail.

Spider decided to try. She made a sack from her webbing, and spun a web to the other side of the world. She was so small that nobody saw her coming. Spider stole a tiny piece of the sun, put it in her sack, and climbed back over her web. Then she said that the sun should be high up in the sky to benefit everyone.

Buzzard said he would carry the sun up into the sky. He placed the sack with the sun in it on his head and flew up to the top of sky. But even in the sack, the sun was very hot and burned off all the feathers on his head and burned the skin underneath red. Still Buzzard flew up until he reached the top of the sky and placed the sun where it would shine on everybody. Ever since, Buzzard has had a bald, red head, but he is honored by all for his sacrifice.

▲ These modern dancers perform a ceremonial dance
at a recent gathering in North Carolina.

An interesting story of the Choctaw of Mississippi tells of a similar "great journey" that their ancestors made from the West, led by two brothers named Chatah and Chikasah. After stopping in a green and bountiful land, the brothers quarreled and the migrating tribe separated into two camps. Instead of fighting, however, the two groups agreed to part in peace, letting a game of chance decide who would stay and who would move on. Chatah and his followers won, so they remained where they were (in Mississippi) and came to be known as the Choctaw. Chikasah's group continued their journey to settle north of their brothers (in Tennessee) as the Chickasaw tribe. Stories such as this show that many Southeastern nations considered themselves as part of one great "family" composed of tribes who originally came from distant areas and spoke different tongues.

## WAYS OF WORSHIP

Because their land had fertile soil and abundant fish, game, and wild plants, the native peoples of the Southeast felt that they had much to be thankful for. Many spirits were often thanked and worshipped for bestowing particular gifts (the sun, for example, for providing light and warmth), but the creator of this great abundance was usually considered to be one all-powerful being. This mighty being was called by many names, depending upon the tribe—"Great One" to the Cherokee, "Giver and Taker of Breath" to the Creek, "Great Spirit" to others. But whatever the name, the creator was worshipped with great seriousness and enthusiasm by the Southeasterners in various rituals.

Ceremonies featuring chants, songs, and dances honored the Great Spirit as well as other spirits responsible for certain "gifts." For instance, among the Creek, dances were of three types—social dances, dances invoking the spirits of certain animals, and busk dances, which were part of the Green Corn Ceremony, also known as *buskita* or *puskita*.

The Green Corn Ceremony enabled the Creek and other Southeastern peoples to celebrate the new season's harvest and offer thanks to the spirit responsible for granting them the all-important gift of corn. This eight-day highlight of the Creek religious and cultural year included fasting and feasting along with the music and dancing. Presided over by a *yakita*, or orator, Green Corn marked the new harvest as a time for

▲ This engraving from 1585 depicts a Southeastern priest participating in a ceremony.

forgiving old grudges and debts and starting life anew. Broken pottery was replaced, new fires were lit, and—in the ceremony's climax—the new corn was eaten for the first time by the community.

In the Seminole version of the Green Corn Ceremony, which lasted from four to six days, the observances included ball games, sweatbaths taken by the holy men, and ritual "scratching" of men and boys with needles, in addition to the fasting, feasting, and dancing. The Yuchi, Shawnee, Choctaw, Cherokee, and Natchez all observed the Green Corn rites, as well.

## CALLING ON THE SPIRITS

For guidance during a hunt or in time of war, or assistance in puberty rites and other ceremonies, the Southeasterners often called upon the spirits

# THE EAGLE DANCE

▲ A Cherokee man describes the importance of the
Eagle Dance to visitors at Oconaluftee Indian Village in
North Carolina.

In 1834 George Catlin provided this vivid description of the Eagle Dance of the Choctaw:

. . . the Eagle Dance . . . is got up by their young men, in honour of that bird, for which they seem to have a religious regard. This picturesque dance was given by twelve or sixteen men, whose bodies were chiefly naked and painted white, with white clay, and each one holding in his hand the tail of the eagle, while his head was also decorated with an eagle's quill. Spears were stuck in the ground, around which the dance was performed by four men at a time, who had simultaneously, at the beat of the drum, jumped up from the ground where they had all sat in rows of four, one row immediately behind the other, and ready to take the place of the first four when they left the ground fatigued, which they did by hopping or jumping around behind the rest, and taking their seats, ready to come up again in their turn, after each of the other sets had been through the same forms.

▲ Three Seminole medicine men pose with Chief Cory Osceola (at right) in Miami, Florida, around 1920. The medicine men wore turbanlike headdresses and a combination of traditional and European-style clothing.

of individual animals through dances, songs, and chants. The Fox Dance of the Creek, for instance, featured women who danced around a fire at an ever-increasing pace, imitating the quickness and slyness of the fox. As part of their Green Corn rites, the Seminole killed a white heron, whose feathers were then held by dancers performing the sacred Feather Dance.

Initiation ceremonies or puberty rites for adolescent Southeasterners often included music and dance. The Chitimacha of Louisiana performed a six-day-long puberty rite in which young men were made to dance until exhausted. Such Carolina tribes as the Congaree and Cheraw required initiates to dance individually—if they were able to remain standing after drinking intoxicating brews administered by priests.

The Southeastern Indians often drank these special brews in solemn ceremonies for strength and courage during war and other endeavors.

One such brew, drunk by the Timucua, Natchez, and other tribes, was a special tea derived from a shrub known as *Ilex vomitoria*, which produced nausea. The sickness caused by this "black drink," as it was often called, was believed to purify the body and spirit of those who drank it. The Creek had a ceremony they called the *asi*, in which adult males drank the black drink from a gourd before war parties, hunts, and sporting contests, and as part of the Green Corn observances, council meetings, and the puberty rites of young men. The black drink, which was brewed from the leaves of a special shrub, was believed by the Creek and the Seminole to be a sacred gift from the Great Spirit. Drinking it was

▲ To purify their bodies and spirits before going to war or participating in ceremonies, Southeastern men often drank a special mixture called the "black drink." The liquid caused the drinker to vomit. In this illustration a priest stands before a war party and prepares to drink the mixture.

a very solemn occasion presided over by the priests of the village.

The priests or holy men of the Southeastern nations (who were nearly always male) held positions of great importance within their tribes. They passed the chants, rituals, and charms, which they themselves had learned through decades of special training by elder priests, on to the next generation. Priests were sometimes known as medicine men and were responsible for preparing herbal remedies and administering them with the proper incantation. The link between the people and the spirits, the medicine man possessed patience, integrity, and, it was believed, powers of healing and clairvoyance. Since the Southeasterners fervently believed that good spirits brought health and prosperity—and that bad spirits brought illness and misfortune—the priest was highly respected and trusted by the community.

Regardless of the occasion, rituals and ceremonies were an integral part of Southeastern Indian life. In addition to seasonal observances (such as Green Corn), preparation for war or the hunt, and rites of puberty and initiation, there were numerous other occasions marked by tribal or village ceremonial gatherings. The Natchez held a ceremony of self-renewal in which the whole village took part. Women and girls danced in a circle around a male singer, waving feathers with one hand and shaking rattles with the other. At the climax of the ceremony, the men and boys struck a symbolic post with their weapons to show loyalty and bravery. Some peoples, such as

▲ Certain Southeastern tribes allowed the bodies of the dead to decompose on open-air platforms. After a year or so, the bones were then ceremonially buried. This illustration from the end of the 16th century shows a burial platform in Virginia.

the Choctaw, performed dances and ceremonies that revolved around games of stickball and other contests. Most tribes also enjoyed social dances, such as the Creek Friendship Dance, which was performed by young, unmarried men and women.

## THE WAYS OF THE DEAD

The most solemn of the Southeastern ceremonies and practices, however, were those designed to lay to rest, mourn, or honor the dead. Some of these burial rituals retained customs and practices of the Mississippian mound-builders of centuries before. In the Gulf Coast region of southern Mississippi, for instance, the Pascagoula and Biloxi tribes preserved the bodies of their deceased leaders and placed them alongside those of their ancestors in earthen temples topped with eternal fires.

▲ In this engraving from 1591, a priest is shown in front of a group of warriors. The priest and many of the men wear round ornaments, or gorgets, on their chests.

The Gulf Coast neighbors of these tribes, the Bayogoula and Chitimacha, shared a different set of burial customs with the Mississippi Choctaw to the north and several other tribes. Instead of burying the dead, the corpse was wrapped and placed on an outdoor platform to dry. After an appropriate interval, specialists known as "bone-pickers," whose fingernails were grown long for the purpose, cleaned the bones of whatever flesh remained. Placed in special baskets, the bones were then set in an honored section of the tribe's bone-house. In the Chitimacha version of

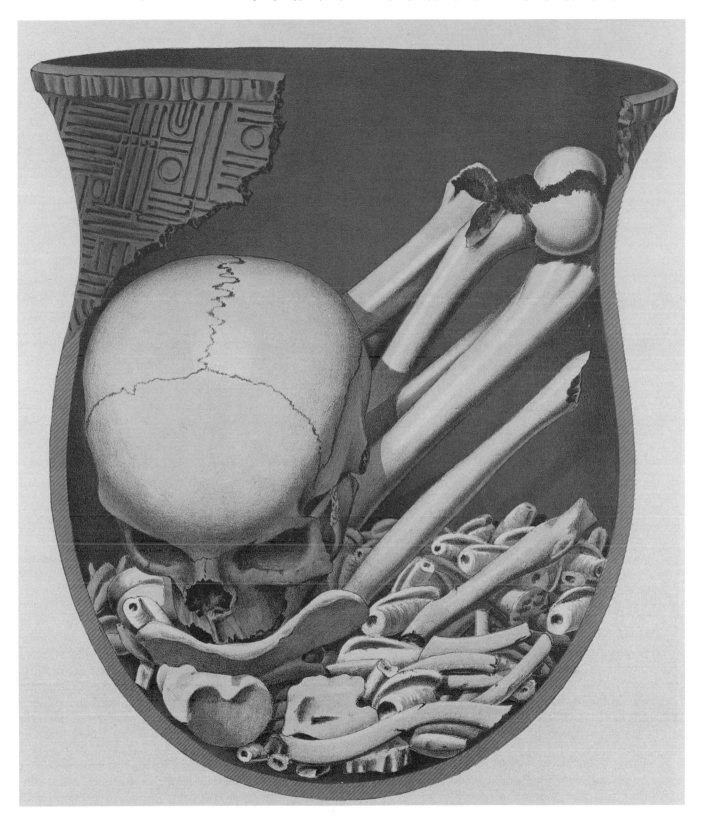

▲ Among some nations of the Southeast, the bones of the dead were placed into pottery containers and buried in funeral mounds. This drawing depicts a burial found on an island off the coast of Georgia.

▲ Indian burial rituals in the post-contact era varied widely among the many Southeastern nations. The Seminole buried the remains of their dead in simply marked graves like the one in this photo, taken in 1906 in Florida.

this custom, an annual ritual was held in which recently buried bodies were removed from their graves and cleaned. The bones were wrapped in a mat and placed in a mound, around which a solemn ceremonial dance was performed.

After paying tribute to their dead through their traditional burial rites, most Southeastern families observed a period of mourning for the deceased. Some tribes, including the Choctaw, held annual retreats in which families mourned all deceased relatives by fasting and covering their heads.

Whether a Southeastern ritual, ceremony, or dance had a serious or lighthearted purpose, the individual rite was carried out with skill and dedication to ancient tribal traditions. The spiritual life has always been of great importance to the Southeastern peoples, and the sense of purpose with which they continue to carry on their tribal ways makes this plain to see.

## THE TOOLS OF THE HOLY MAN

During the long years (often as many as 20) he spent mastering his sacred craft, the Southeastern priest or medicine man learned to use a wide variety of objects, believed to contain spiritual powers, to summon good spirits and drive away bad ones. These objects ranged from charms worn on the body to rattles made from gourds or hides. Charms and fetishes (carved objects representing spirits or sacred animals) fashioned from stone, bone, animal teeth, or feathers were considered to possess great powers. Such items were highly valued and their exact nature was often kept secret. Stone charms were often worn as necklaces by the medicine men. Amulets of polished quartz were particularly prized by the Cherokee.

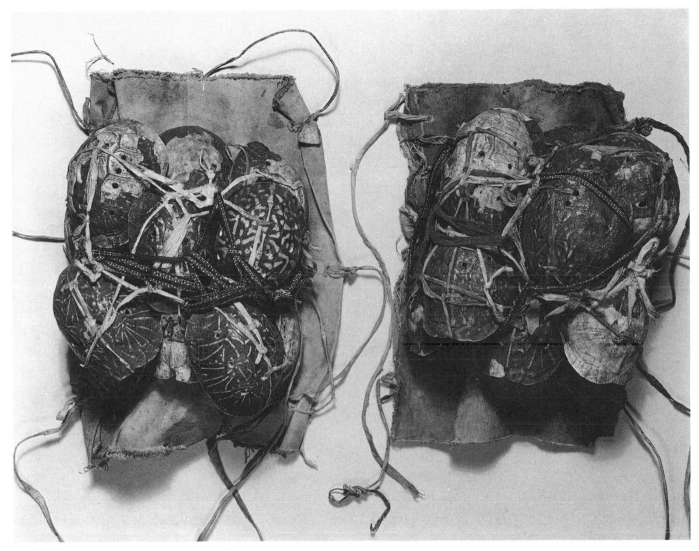

▲ To make rattles, Southeastern Native Americans filled turtle shells with pebbles. In this example, the shells have been attached to pieces of cloth, which were then tied around the arms or legs of a dancer.

Among the most sacred possessions of a tribal holy man were what the non-Indians somewhat inaccurately called "medicine bundles"—animal hides that were wrapped around the tribe's most powerful and spiritual objects. A smaller, personal version of the medicine bundle, known as a medicine pouch, was worn by individuals throughout most of North America. Because of their sacred status and great spiritual powers, the Southeasterners' medicine bundles were carefully guarded and only brought out when needed for treating the sick or conducting a ritual or ceremony. In the Green Corn rites of the Seminole, for example, the medicine bundles are brought out by the holy man on the morning of the third

day, opened to reveal their contents only during that night's rituals, and hidden again at dawn.

Other important items among the Southeastern holy man's spiritual tools included a stone medicine tube, used to administer herbal medicine to a patient by blowing or sucking; rattles (made from gourds or hides among such inland tribes as the Cherokee, or from turtle shells among coastal peoples, including the Creek and Seminole), either hand-held or strapped to the legs; and the ceremonial pipe, or calumet—a particularly sacred object to native peoples throughout the Americas. The term *calumet* actually refers only to the long, often-decorated wooden stem of the pipe but later came to denote

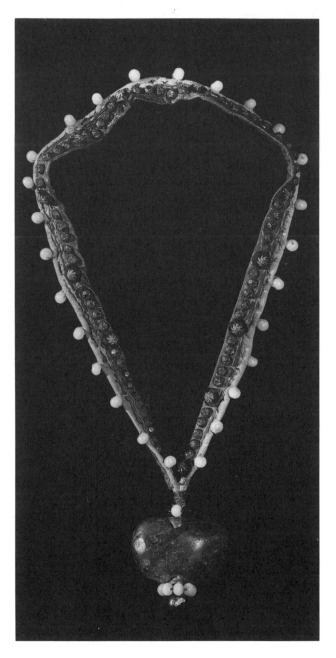

▲ This Cherokee amulet is made from a piece of polished quartz attached to a beaded strap. Amulets such as this were worn around the neck and had great personal significance to their owners.

the entire pipe. Because smoking it at the signing of peace treaties was popular among tribes of the Plains and elsewhere, the calumet has been usually recognized as a symbol of peace. In the Southeast, however, the calumet has long been smoked by holy men in such tribes as the Creek, Chitimacha, and others as an offering to the spirits in sacred ceremonies.

## A TIME FOR PLAY

Work, worship, and war were among the major occupations of the Southeastern Indians, but they often found time to play, too. Members of virtually every Southeastern nation took part in a variety of games and athletic contests between individuals, villages, and even entire tribes. Such games ranged from stickball—an exhilarating and widely popular team sport played throughout the region—to contests of skill and various games of chance. Dice games were especially popular among Southeastern women, who used a wide range of objects for dice: dried corn (Choctaw), cane (Natchez), lima beans (Cherokee), and fruit seeds.

In general, the Southeasterners referred to their games as "the little brother of war," and with good reason. Their athletic contests were rough-and-tumble affairs, played with great enthusiasm and ferocity—and with little regard for the safety of players, who took their games very seriously. Stickball, the best-known and most widely played game of the region, is a perfect example of native Southeastern ingenuity and athletic endeavor.

## STICKBALL AND OTHER GAMES

Stickball—which French explorers called *la crosse*, because the playing sticks reminded them of a bishop's staff—is basically a simple game that can be played by a great number of people at one time but requires only a few items of equipment to play. Each player carries two wooden sticks or rackets, each with a loop crossed by leather thongs at the end. The object of the game is for each of two teams to move a deerskin ball (about the size of a golf ball) down an outdoor field about 500 feet long and through the opposing team's goalposts a certain number of times.

The particulars of stickball—the styles of the rackets and goalposts, the length of the field, the number of players involved and goals required to win, and the stakes—varied from tribe to tribe, but the basic game remained the same and was played by most Southeastern nations. Most tribes had a rule that players must pick up, carry, and throw the ball only with their sticks and must not touch it with their hands.

The Catawba of South Carolina, for example, played under the "no hands" rule with rackets

# STICKBALL AMONG THE CHOCTAW

The American artist George Catlin (1796–1872) visited many Native American peoples in the 1830s. He took many notes and made numerous sketches and paintings that today are an important source of information about the various tribes. In 1834 he described a stickball game played by a group of Choctaw:

This wonderful game . . . can never be appreciated by those who are not happy enough to see it.

It is no uncommon experience for six or eight hundred or a thousand of these young men, to engage in a game of ball, with five or six times that number of spectators, of men, women, and children, surrounding the ground, and looking on. . . .

The sticks with which this tribe play, are bent into an oblong loop at the end, with a sort of slight web of small thongs tied across, to prevent the ball from passing through. The players hold one of these in each hand, and by leaping into the air, they catch the ball between the two nettings and throw it, without being allowed to strike it, or catch it in their hands.

▲ The Choctaw, Cherokee, Catawba, and other Southeastern tribes all played the Indian game of stickball with great enthusiasm. The stick used to move the ball around the field, seen here, is made of hickory.

made from solid sticks of wood shaped like large spoons; the Cherokee usually played until one team scored 12 times. Since stickball games were often important events where the prestige and standing of a village or tribe were at stake, the players took great pains to prepare themselves to win. The entire village would come out to take part in the team's preparation ceremonies and to root for the players on the field.

Cherokee stickball players observed a week-long period of pre-game rituals, including fasting, dances, scratchings, paintings, and incantations administered by the medicine man to summon the power of the spirits. The stickball traditions of the Choctaw were among the most elaborate, colorful, and long-standing of those of the Southeastern tribes, and the game is still immensely popular among young Choctaw in both their native Mississippi and in Oklahoma, where most reside today.

A game of Southeastern-style stickball as played by the Choctaw was a wild event that gave the men a chance to blow off steam in a relatively safe way. Swift, muscular players fought each other to advance the ball downfield at top speed while medicine men moved among them, beckoning the spirits to aid their team. The American writer and artist George Catlin, who described and painted numerous scenes of Choctaw stickball games in the Indian Territory (Oklahoma) in the 1830s, summed up the exhilaration of Southeastern stickball in this way: "This wonderful game . . . can never be appreciated by those who are not happy enough to see it."

Although it did not enjoy the widespread popularity of stickball in the Southeast, the game of chunkey was also played in various versions throughout the region. Played by only two

people at a time on an outdoor court or yard, chunkey consists of throwing a long pole (resembling a javelin) at a smooth, rounded stone that was rolled along the ground. Chunkey was played with great enthusiasm by, among others, the Creek, Mugulasha, and Bayogoula of the Gulf Coast, and the Choctaw. It is still played today by some of the Choctaw remaining in Mississippi.

## WAR

The waging of war was a fact of life among Native American tribes, as it has always been among most nations of the world. The tribes of the Southeast were no exception to this rule. Aside from fighting to protect their lands, homes, and families from attack by rival tribes, some Southeastern groups often made war when there were no territorial issues or questions of survival at stake. Men referred to war as their "beloved occupation," an activity to be relished after the work of providing food and shelter for their families was taken care of.

It may at first appear strange that the Southeastern culture—with its highly respected religious, community, and governmental practices, well-developed arts and crafts, abundance of food, and comfortable standard of living—would find war anything other than a means of preserving its way of life. History shows, however, that prosperous, "advanced" nations—including the United States—are the ones that can most afford to maintain a standing army whose sole purpose

▲ War was called the "beloved occupation" by many Southeastern tribes. In a somewhat fanciful illustration made by a European in the late 1500s, Southeastern men "declare war" on a fenced village by placing arrows in the ground.

is to wage war. The Southeastern tribes fit this description; they were indeed prosperous and usually did not fight to conquer the territory or enslave the inhabitants of neighboring tribes. What appealed to many Southeastern men were the challenge, skill, courage, and risks involved in war.

With longbows, knives, and large warclubs as weapons, Southeastern warriors usually raided the village of an enemy at night. Moving quietly through the darkness, a war party would sneak up on the unsuspecting village, suddenly attack, sometimes setting homes afire, and shooting or clubbing the terrified inhabitants as they fled. Warriors often favored clubs and other hand weapons over the bow and arrow, since their use

required a closer range and more risk, thereby displaying greater courage. Courage was an essential part of the psychology of warfare, and proving it involved some of the grislier aspects of Southeastern warfare—namely, the taking of trophies and the torture of captives.

The taking of enemy scalps was an age-old custom among Iroquois warriors in the Northeast but was spread throughout the continent by the Europeans who invaded Indian lands. In order to take a scalp or a limb as a trophy, a warrior had to successfully engage in hand-to-hand combat with an enemy, showing great courage. And since the capturing or killing of non-combatants, including women and children, required the skillful and courageous entry into the enemy's homes, such actions were permissible in war.

However, if a warrior was unlucky enough to be captured alive by an enemy—the Natchez, for example—his courage would be put to the ultimate test; he would most likely be tortured to

death in a public ritual that the villagers often performed with relish. While the captive taunted his tormentors with a defiant "death song," the torturers—who were most often women—did whatever they could to break his spirit before he finally succumbed.

One important aspect of the custom of torturing captives—regardless of its apparent cruelty—was the respect that the torturers gave to their victim's bravery if he strove to prove his courage and maintain his dignity regardless of what his captors did to him. It is also important to point out that this practice was usually limited to enemy warriors and often pales in comparison to the mass torture and slaughter that European invaders regularly carried out against Native American men, women, and children.

The torture of captive warriors and the ferocity with which the Southeastern nations often waged war can be puzzling when one looks at other aspects of the Southeasterners' culture. These tribes were also kind, hardworking, loving, and reverent peoples. Their individual members valued human life and the loss of a loved one in battle was not an easy thing to bear. One theory among historians holds that the torture custom, usually only practiced on adult male warriors, may have begun as a village's means of avenging its dead after a battle. The ritual held religious significance as well because prayers were often recited, giving thanks for the captive and offering his courage as a gift to the spirits.

The institution of war played an important role in the culture of most Southeastern tribes, some of whom—the Cherokee, for instance—pointed with pride at their ability and enjoyment of war. It had its place in their lives, and some tribes admittedly enjoyed it, but war was not all that they lived for. They fought to protect their homes and families from their enemies but not often to conquer. The domination of other peoples was not a common occurrence among the Southeastern nations. The main concern of the Indians of the region was similar to that of many cultures past and present—to live, freely and undisturbed, on land that had been theirs for centuries.

They worked their land, gave thanks for all they had, and enjoyed life as much as they could. They traded with each other and fought each other from time to time. When they first encountered the light-skinned visitors who suddenly appeared on their lands in the 16th century, the Southeastern tribes did not automatically treat

▲ This European portrait of a young Seminole, armed with bow, arrows, and shield, dates from the 1840s. It illustrates the Southeastern belief that warfare is a noble pursuit.

the Europeans as intruders to be repulsed. Instead, nations such as the Creek, Cherokee, Powhatan, and many others often welcomed the strangers from across the sea, sharing their food and shelter with them and helping them to survive in a hostile environment—charitable acts that many of the Southeasterners would later have cause to regret. The Europeans' survival in their "new world," which they owed in part to the hospitality of Native Americans, would forever change the lives and futures of the peoples of the Southeast.

# CEREMONIAL LIFE

✶ ✶ ✶ ✶ ✶ ✶ ✶ ✶ ✶ ✶ ✶ ✶ ✶

## SACRED SITES

▼ The beautiful spring of pure water found at Red Clay in Tennessee is considered sacred by the Cherokee.

✶ ✶ ✶ ✶ ✶ ✶ ✶ ✶ ✶ ✶ ✶ ✶ ✶

# BOOGER MASKS

* * * * * * * * * * * * *

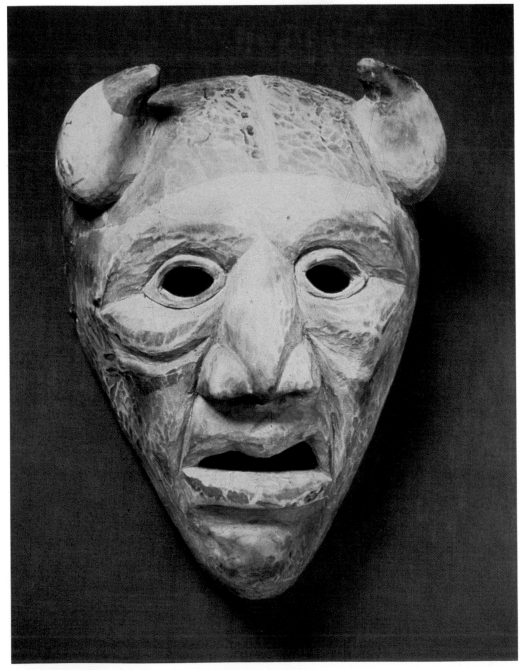

▲ Cherokee Booger masks were meant to be frightening. This wooden mask has carved horns on the forehead and may represent the fierce water monster Uktena. The influence of African-American slaves on the Indians of the Southeast is seen in Booger masks, which are related to the African tradition of the bogeyman, or evil spirit.

▲ The face of this Cherokee Booger mask is made of carved and painted wood. The hair, eyebrows, mustache, and beard are made of animal fur. Because the face is painted black and because Native American men had little facial hair, this mask may represent an African-American.

# RITUAL OBJECTS

\* \* \* \* \* \* \* \* \* \* \* \* \*

◀ This modern painting by Creek/Cherokee artist Joan Hill represents an ancient Creek ceremonial figure in full regalia. He wears a deer headdress, a feather cloak, a necklace of bear claws, and carries a ritual staff.

▶ This ceremonial Seminole rattle is made from palmetto leaves.

▼ Priests or shamans wore special clothing for ceremonies. This shaman's outfit was worn by a Seminole.

\* \* \* \* \* \* \* \* \* \* \* \* \*

# DANCE

* * * * * * * * * * * * * *

▲ Dancing has been a part of Native American culture for thousands of years, whether performed in a serious religious rite or a lighthearted celebration. Here, a Choctaw dancer at a festival in Alabama swirls around in his brilliant feathered costume, more reminiscent of Plains Indian style than traditional Choctaw dress.

▲ Dressed in a traditional smock of vivid red, a Cherokee musician solemnly beats the drum for a ceremonial dance at a Tennessee Indian festival.

▲ A Southeastern Indian dancer, in full ceremonial dress, stops to take a drink during a Tennessee Indian festival.

# CHAPTER FOUR

✳ ✳ ✳ ✳ ✳ ✳ ✳ ✳ ✳ ✳ ✳ ✳ ✳

# CHANGE

ntil the middle of the 16th century, the peoples inhabiting the Southeastern portion of the North American continent had lived, traded, and fought with each other without interference from visitors of other races. Although a nation would occasionally be defeated by and absorbed into a stronger neighboring tribe— as probably happened with the Mississippian Cultures around A.D. 1300—through it all, most tribes managed to maintain their own identities and their own lands.

At the time of Christopher Columbus's first voyages in the 1490s, there were more than a score of major Indian nations and confederacies controlling various sections of the Southeast, in a wide arc stretching from the Gulf of Mexico, along the Mississippi and Ohio rivers, north and eastward to Chesapeake Bay. In the southwest corner of the region, near the Gulf Coast and along the lower Mississippi, were the Louisiana region tribes—the Chitimacha, Bayogoula, Tunica, Natchez and, stretching westward into Texas and Arkansas, the Atakapa and the Caddo Confederacy.

Mississippi was home to the Biloxi in the south, the Choctaw and Yazoo in the center and, in the north, the Chickasaw, whose range also extended north across the western portions of Tennessee and Kentucky. The southern portion of

what is now Alabama was home to the Mobile and, naturally, the Alabama. Most of Tennessee (and parts of northern Georgia and western North Carolina) was Cherokee territory. Present-day Virginia was home to the tribes of the Powhatan Confederacy; eastern North Carolina to the Tuscarora; and South Carolina to the Catawba and several other tribes.

Part of eastern Georgia was occupied by the Yuchi, with the Yamasee farther to the south. The Florida peninsula was originally inhabited by the Timucua in the northeastern and central regions, the Ais on the Atlantic coast, the Calusa on the southern Gulf Coast, the Apalachee in the north (near Tallahassee), and the Pensacola in the northwest, on the Panhandle. In time, all would vanish, and only an offshoot of the Creek, called the Seminole, would remain in Florida.

The most powerful of the Southeastern nations, however, was a confederacy of tribes stretching across most of Alabama and Georgia and calling themselves the Muskogee. These tribes included the Hitchiti and Tuskegee, among others. British traders referred to them as the "Indians of the Creek"—and as the Creek Confederacy, they controlled much of the Southeast.

## THE EUROPEANS ARRIVE

An expedition led by the Spanish governor of Puerto Rico, Juan Ponce de León, to find a place called "Bimini" and a legendary "fountain of youth," resulted in the first contact between native North Americans and Europeans in 1513. The Spanish group arrived in Florida and explored much of the coast but were prevented from establishing a settlement by the fierce resistance of the Calusa in the first recorded clash between whites and Native Americans on North American soil. Finding no "fountain," Ponce de León returned to Puerto Rico. In 1521 he returned to Florida to try again; this time, he was mortally wounded in battle and his second attempt at colonization failed. So did two subsequent Spanish expeditions in 1526 and 1528. During this period, Spanish slave ships made occasional raids along Florida's Gulf Coast to abduct Native Americans into slavery; however, another decade would pass before the Europeans would again attempt to push inland to explore and establish settlements in the Southeast.

The first successful European exploration of the North American continent began on May 28, 1539, when a Spanish invasion force commanded by Hernando de Soto—wealthy and fresh from helping Francisco Pizarro conquer the Inca of Peru—landed at Tampa Bay, on Florida's Gulf Coast. Motivated by rumors of great riches to be found in the interior, de Soto's well-equipped army made a circuitous route throughout most of the Southeast over the next three years. Hoping to find gold, the Spanish invaders encountered few treasures but instead met with considerable resistance from local Indians, who remembered the slavers.

Although most of the Indians fought de Soto's soldiers to protect their own lands and people, other native Southeasterners, including some among the Natchez and Creek, gave the Spaniards help and guidance as they made their way into the heart of the region. In some cases, Native Americans were forced into assisting de Soto's forces by threats or imprisonment; in others, they may have been interested in Spanish weaponry and technology, or perhaps were simply curious about the culture of their uninvited guests. In any case, the Spaniards did receive Native American help in their explorations.

Often, however, the native peoples' reward for their cooperation was enslavement, or worse. De Soto earned a reputation as being "much given to the sport of slaying Indians." His forces pushed their way north through the Florida peninsula into Georgia and the Carolinas; westward and southward again through Tennessee and down

▲ The Native Americans of the Southeast first came into contact with Europeans in the 16th century. In this engraving from 1591, a European carrying a sword sits with a Timucua priest in northern Florida. The priest's body is decorated with tatoos.

the Alabama River toward Mobile; northwest into Mississippi and across the Mississippi River (becoming the first whites to "discover" and cross it), and even into Arkansas and Louisiana before de Soto himself died of a fever in 1542.

De Soto's invasion effectively opened the Southeast to European exploration, and its tribes to prolonged contact with whites. The de Soto expedition encountered, among others, the Calusa, Timucua, Creek, Cherokee, Choctaw, Chickasaw, and Natchez—in fact, most of the major Southeastern tribes—and signaled the coming of profound changes in their lives.

## UNINVITED GUESTS

Not long after de Soto's journey, Europeans began trickling into the Southeast. Within 25 years of de Soto's death, settlements had been established in Florida by France (Fort Caroline, 1564) and Spain (St. Augustine, 1565). Spain soon gained control of Florida and began sending

# THE EUROPEAN VIEWPOINT

One of the very first Europeans to record the life-style of the Native Americans of the Southeast was the French artist Jacques Le Moyne, who traveled to Florida in 1564. His depictions of the Timucua were published in 1591. Because the Timucua were virtually wiped out by the 17th century, Le Moyne's illustrations are a valuable source of information about this tribe and about Southeastern tribes in general. The pictures must be viewed with caution, however, because Le Moyne gives the Native Americans many European characteristics. In this illustration, for example, an important chief named Outina (at left) is shown going to war at the head of troops marching in a European hollow-square formation. The spear he carries has a metal point. In fact, warriors in the Southeast marched single file and their spears had stone tips. A very accurate detail is the sharply pointed fingernail Outina displays on his left hand. Warriors filed their nails into points in order to gouge their enemies' foreheads and blind them with blood.

explorers and missionaries north into Georgia and west along the Gulf Coast toward Louisiana. Although the original Spanish expeditions in the area had mainly sought land and gold, the Spaniards later concentrated their efforts on "converting"—often with brutality—the native peoples they encountered to the Roman Catholic faith. Over time, the Spanish missionaries in Florida succeeded in converting many Indians to Christianity.

The first British colony in North America, at Jamestown, Virginia, was established in 1607. By the 1640s—a century after de Soto—other English settlements had taken root in Virginia and the Carolinas (as well as in the Northeast). In 1682, Robert La Salle had claimed the lower Mississippi valley for France; in 1699, the first French settlement was established at Biloxi. The 17th century was drawing to a close, and the Europeans had arrived.

When the three major European powers active in the Southeast—England, Spain, and France—began to colonize what they called the New World in the 16th and 17th centuries, they brought with them goods, weapons, attitudes, rivalries, and practices that would have a dramatic effect on the Native Americans of the Southeast.

The Indians looked upon these intruders with a mixture of caution and curiosity. They had seen the Spaniards kill many of their people or carry them off to slavery and so were not quick to trust many Europeans. Yet the visitors possessed weapons and tools—especially guns and knives—that made hunting and farming (not to mention warfare) far more efficient, and beautiful fabrics, hats, shoes, and other articles of clothing. What was more, the strangers were eager to trade these goods for animal skins, which the Southeasterners were particularly good at obtaining.

## TRADERS AND ALLIES

All three rival European powers in the region sent traders to try to influence the chiefs of the tribes, presenting them with gifts of goods and attempting to persuade them to do business with whatever country they represented. Such tactics often worked, and many Southeastern nations entered into what they saw as profitable relationships with the European traders.

From these trading partnerships, a number of powerful political and military alliances developed between Southeastern nations and the representatives of the European powers. The various

▲ Timucua Indians of Florida shuttle crops to a public granary in this 1564 engraving by Frenchman Jacques Le Moyne.

tribes found the friendship and aid of their new allies especially helpful when a conflict arose with a traditional enemy. But these alliances both helped and hindered the Southeasterners in preserving and protecting their ancestral land—largely because of the growing dependence of the tribes on European guns and goods, and the frequently shifting balance of power among the colonies and their parent nations.

Trailing somewhat behind the Spanish and British in colonizing the Southeast, the French were nonetheless established in the Mississippi delta by the beginning of the 18th century. The Choctaw, whose territory lay close to the settlements of Mobile, Biloxi, and New Orleans, traded and eventually formed an alliance with the French. In contrast, the Chickasaw—traditional enemies of the Choctaw—aligned themselves with the British, who were enemies of France. To the north, however, the Cherokee managed to carry on relatively friendly relations with both powers, at least for a time.

The Creek, for their part, excelled at diplomacy, a skill that was particularly helpful considering their geographical position. Creek lands were bordered by all three European powers—the Spanish to the south (in Florida), the French to the south and west (along the northern Gulf Coast) and the British to the north and east (in coastal Georgia, the Carolinas, and Virginia). The

Creek Confederacy was a large group of related tribes, rather than one united nation, and its individual members were quite skilled at playing along with the European traders and representatives who sought their business and political support by showering them with gifts. Their skill in the diplomatic arts enabled them to stay one step ahead of the Europeans, pitting one rival power against another.

The native Southeasterners generally welcomed the new technologies that the Europeans introduced to their lands—firearms, iron and steel implements, a variety of woven fabrics—and were eager to trade for these goods. The increased protection from neighboring hostile tribes that an alliance with the Europeans could provide was also highly valued by the Indians. Not so welcome, however, were a number of more dubious "gifts" that the colonists brought with them from the Old World and whose effects they spread among the Southeastern peoples: brutally enforced European religion, slavery, disease, alcohol and—perhaps most destructive of all—an overwhelming greed for land.

## POWHATAN'S WISDOM

A number of Southeastern nations—including some who had been more than cooperative with their foreign visitors—found rather early in their relationships with Europeans that there was indeed a reason for caution. Powhatan (whose given name was Wahunsonacock), chief of the powerful Powhatan Confederacy, which controlled much of Virginia and the northeastern corner of North Carolina, was among the first Native American leaders to deal extensively with European intruders. When the first English settlers established the colony of Jamestown in 1607, Powhatan initially regarded them with suspicion. The great chief would have had Captain John Smith of Jamestown executed in 1608 had it not been for the now-legendary intervention of his daughter, Pocahontas, who asked him to spare Smith's life.

Following that episode, Powhatan attempted to carry on friendly relations with the Jamestown colonists, and his tribe's assistance enabled the settlers to survive some very hard times. The chief, however, soon found the English to be more interested in acquiring his lands and goods than in simply enjoying his people's hospitality. In the following 1609 speech, recorded by Captain Smith himself, Powhatan questions the wisdom of the colonists' hostility and warns of the possible consequences:

> Why should you take by force from us that which you can have by love? Why should you destroy us, who have provided you with food? What can you get by war? We can hide our provisions and fly into the woods; and then you must consequently famish by wronging your friends. What is the cause of your jealousy? You see us unarmed, and willing to supply your wants, if you will come in a friendly manner, and not with swords and guns, as to invade an enemy.
>
> I am not so simple, as to know it is better to eat good meat, lie well, and sleep quietly with my women and children; to laugh and be merry with the English; and, being their friend, to have copper, hatchets, and whatever else I want, than to fly from all, to lie cold in the woods, food upon acorns, roots and such trash, and to be so hunted, that I cannot rest, eat, or sleep. In such circumstances, my men must watch, and if a twig should but break, all would cry out, "Here comes Captain Smith;" and so, in this miserable manner, to end my miserable life; and, Captain Smith, this might soon be your fate too, through your rashness and unadvisedness.
>
> I, therefore, exhort you to peaceable councils; and, above all, I insist that the guns and swords, the cause of all our jealousy and uneasiness, be removed and sent away.

Powhatan's impassioned and prophetic plea appeared to have fallen on deaf ears, since the Jamestown colonists—after crowning the great chief "emperor"—turned around and tried to capture him the following year (1610). Three years later his beloved daughter, Pocahontas, was abducted by colonists and held for ransom, although she was later released in exchange for English prisoners. Pocahontas subsequently fell in love with and married Jamestown colonist John Rolfe. Their union helped keep the peace. Within a few years she returned with Rolfe to England, where she was received as royalty but died of smallpox in 1617.

After Powhatan himself died a year later, the English renewed hostilities; Powhatan's brother Opitchipan, who had succeeded him, had

enough and finally led his warriors against the Jamestown colonists. War raged on, with "massacres" occurring on both sides, for 15 years, but the growing colony was eventually able to outman and outgun the Powhatan. By 1634, fulfilling its late chief 's prophecy, the once-mighty Powhatan Confederacy—once numbering nearly 9,000 strong—was all but wiped out by the Jamestown forces. It was among the first of many Southeastern Native American nations to be vanquished by the same European colonists it had once helped to survive.

## A LEGACY OF MISFORTUNE

The steady stream of European colonists arriving on North American soil during the 17th and 18th centuries brought drastic changes to the lives of Indians wherever the colonists settled. In the Southeast, the tribes of the Florida peninsula and the eastern Gulf Coast were among the first to feel the effects of European expansion from the Spanish colonies in that area. Soon the English began to colonize the Atlantic coast and the French moved down into the Mississippi Valley from Canada. In each case, the intruders brought more with them than just goods to trade. They brought alcohol; they brought an insatiable desire for land and the firearms to help them get it; and more often than not—and perhaps without realizing it, at least at first—they brought deadly disease to the Southeastern peoples.

Smallpox—a frightful infectious disease that killed millions of Europeans—decimated the Native American population as well between 1600 and 1800. Other illnesses brought into North America by the whites, including cholera, mumps, and measles, overwhelmed the Indians, who had no immunity to them and no way to treat them effectively. Some estimates, in fact, put the percentage of Native Americans killed by European diseases in certain areas of the Southeast (such as in the Carolinas) at around 85 percent in just 50 years—roughly between 1650 and 1700. Small tribes were hit the hardest. One particular example is the Sewee of South Carolina, a tribe whose people had numbered about 800 at the beginning of the 17th century but dwindled, mainly due to smallpox, to about 50 by 1700— less than 50 years after the first English colonists arrived in the area. Larger Southeastern tribes, too, were vulnerable to such epidemics. The Cherokee, for example, often suffered greatly from smallpox, and the victims frequently

▲ This 17th-century engraving depicts the great Virginia Indian chief Wahunsonacock—popularly known as Powhatan—presiding over the people of the Powhatan Confederacy.

jumped into rivers and streams to relieve the disease's painful rash, only to die from the shock to their bodies.

In Tennessee and the Carolinas, the Catawba tribe, with a population that once peaked at nearly 5,000, fell victim to a combination of unfortunate circumstances brought about by contact with Europeans—including slavery, war, alcohol, disease, and dependence on the colonists. These effects represented a pattern repeated among many tribes throughout the Southeast. After extensive trading with colonists in the late 17th century, Catawba warriors applied their fighting abilities to the use of firearms, becoming quite adept at European-style warfare and much feared among other Southeastern tribes.

When the English colonists in the Carolinas attempted to enslave them around 1715, the

Catawba joined forces with the neighboring Yamasee and went to war against the colonists. They were defeated by the English, with casualties running into the thousands. Over the next 60 years or so, the weakened Catawba suffered from recurring epidemics, widespread alcoholism, and repeated attacks by stronger enemies until, by 1775, their number had been reduced to only 400. The Catawba had been virtually wiped out within a century or so of their first contact with Europeans. Although the time required varied from tribe to tribe, this very same fate awaited most of the other Southeastern nations, with a few notable exceptions.

## CAUGHT IN THE WHITE MAN'S WARS

The gradual destruction of most of the Southeastern Indian nations was a direct result of European colonial policies (and, later, of policies of the United States government). In Florida, where the Calusa, Appalachee, and Timucua once thrived, Spain carried on a program of brutal "religious conversion," enslavement, and conquest of all three tribes after St. Augustine was founded in 1565. Spain's ongoing frontier wars with Britain throughout the 17th and 18th centuries also contributed to the downfall of the original Florida tribes. The Appalachee (whose name is the basis for the term *Appalachian*) were all but destroyed in a raid by British colonial forces operating against Spanish colonists in 1704; nearly 8,000 Indians were killed, captured, or carried into slavery. After most of the Timucua had been converted to Catholicism by the Spaniards, English raids greatly reduced their number, and by the 1740s the tribe had all but vanished.

The Calusa, by contrast, had maintained their tribal identity despite widespread conquest and conversion by the Spanish since the mid-1500s but were later removed by the English after they gained control of Florida in the 1760s. Around 1800, an offshoot of the Creek Confederacy called the Seminole moved into the territory that once belonged to the earlier Florida tribes and absorbed the remnants of those tribes into their own population. The Seminole later waged a bitter struggle with the U.S. government to remain in Florida; the "Seminole Wars" were fought on and off for nearly all the first half of the 19th century. Although most Seminole were eventually removed against their will to Indian Territory,

many reside on Florida reservations to this day. A small number of them, although actually peaceful, are still technically at war with the United States, never having signed an official agreement of surrender.

A fate similar to that of the Florida tribes befell the Natchez and the Houma of the western Gulf Coast and lower Mississippi Valley around 1730; this time, however, conquest came at the hands of French colonists and their Choctaw allies, who raided both the Natchez and Houma, capturing thousands and selling them into slavery. Remnants of the Natchez fled north and settled among the Chickasaw, Creek, and Cherokee, while all but a few of the Houma disappeared within a decade.

By the middle of the 18th century, only a handful of strong Southeastern nations had survived the ravages of European colonial expansion, disease, dependence, and alcohol relatively intact—the Cherokee, Creek, Choctaw, and Chickasaw. During this period the political strength of the surviving Southeastern tribes allied with one or another of the European colonial powers reached its peak. Chiefs of the Creek and Cherokee, for example, occasionally traveled to London as official representatives of their people to confer with the king of England. Traders and representatives of the colonies frequently married into the tribes, and their offspring often became Indian statesmen, princes, or landowners.

The major Indian nations enjoyed a measure of prosperity during this period, and many of their people adopted European-style clothing, homes, and agricultural methods, acquired livestock, and raised horses. But although in outward appearance they may have resembled their European allies, most Southeasterners still practiced and maintained tribal traditions in their ceremonies, festivals, games, and preparations for war.

In the midst of this prosperity for the Southeastern nations, the centuries-old rivalry between the French and English came to a showdown in the New World when war broke out in 1754, in a conflict often referred to as the French and Indian War. Disputes over territorial borders, trading rights with the Indians, and a recently built line of French forts triggered the fighting, which dragged on for nearly a decade and involved most of the major Southeastern tribes.

Although they often had disputes with the British off and on during the 1750s, the Cherokee still fought alongside the British and the Chicka-

saw in their struggle with the French. The conflict finally ended in an English victory—and in the cession of most French holdings in North America—in 1763. In return for their assistance to Britain, these nations received assurances that their lands from the Appalachians to the Mississippi would be closed to white settlement—although this promise, like so many others, would never actually be honored. Even the Creek, whose diplomatic skill allowed them to court both sides of the conflict, received continued aid from the British for their help.

Tribes allied with the French, however—such as the Choctaw and several tribes in the Creek Confederacy—suddenly found themselves without a European ally after 1763. As a result of the war, France lost Canada and all of its lands east of the Mississippi to Britain, while French holdings west of the Mississippi—the vast Louisiana Territory—had been secretly ceded to Spain during the war. And Spain had turned Florida over to the British as well. France was now completely out of the picture in the Southeast, and its major Indian allies, the Choctaw, could no longer count on its protection. Since the Choctaw did not actually take up arms against the British during the war, however, their lands in Mississippi were relatively safe—at least for the moment.

Some nations east of the Mississippi that had been friendly to the French—including such Creek tribes as the Coushatta and groups from the Alabama, Biloxi, Tunica, Pascagoula, and Choctaw tribes, and a few remaining Houma and Appalachee—moved westward across the river to be closer to the French settlers who would remain in Louisiana and away from the English. And so, with settlers from the victorious British colonies preparing to push westward toward the Mississippi and lands formerly held by the French, the stage was now set for the next great event that would further disrupt the lives of the Southeastern peoples and present them with yet another challenge: the American Revolution.

## CHALLENGE FROM A NEW REPUBLIC

As the first shots in the American Revolution were being fired in Massachusetts in 1775, the Southeastern Indian nations were unsure about what the Revolution might mean to them and their ancient lands. Some, including bands of young Cherokee warriors, felt that this was the time to strike against the infant country in such frontier areas as Tennessee, to prevent the Americans' further expansion into Indian lands. Others, such as Cherokee leader Nancy Ward, the "Beloved Woman" of the Cherokee, believed that the only way for the Southeastern nations to survive was to peacefully adjust to and coexist with white Americans and their brand-new country.

In July of 1777, a Cherokee war party did plan an attack on the Tennessee frontier but was repulsed by the frontier militia. As a result, the Cherokee surrendered Tennessee land to the United States, in a treaty establishing a boundary that was to remain "through all generations," the first of hundreds of treaties that white Americans would sign with the Native Americans during the coming century, and then, with an eye toward westward expansion, proceed to ignore.

During the Revolution itself, the Cherokee and Choctaw followed a policy of friendly neutrality toward the United States, but the Chickasaw, in an effort to prevent their ancient hunting grounds from falling into the hands of Northern Indians friendly to the British, actually fought against their former British allies alongside the United States. After the war, both the Choctaw and Chickasaw signed treaties with the new American republic that formally defined the boundaries of their tribal lands. The Creek Confederacy, however, maintained friendly relations with the British throughout the war, which ended with the American victory at Yorktown in 1783.

The establishment of the United States posed a new challenge in the Southeasterners' struggle to maintain the integrity of their ancestral lands against the rush of settlers who were poised to begin moving west. To meet this challenge, a number of great Native American statesmen and leaders appeared on the scene to represent the Southeastern Indian nations at the treaty table and promote unity among the tribes and nations. One of these was Alexander McGillivray, a brilliant Creek statesman who sought formal recognition of the Creek Confederacy (in present-day Georgia and Alabama) as an independent nation from Spain and Great Britain as well as from the United States. Basing his strategy upon Thomas Jefferson's Northwest Ordinance of 1787 (which stated that the U.S. government can take no land from Indians without their consent), McGillivray was on the verge of securing formal recognition for the Creek nation from Spain when he died in 1793, leaving the Creek Confederacy without its

# SEQUOYAH AND HIS SYLLABARY

Among the achievements of the Cherokee Indians during the period from 1814 through the 1830s was the development and adoption of the first written alphabet for a Native American language—the Cherokee Syllabary devised by Sequoyah (1776–1843), son of a Cherokee chief's daughter and a white officer of the American Revolution. After having problems with alcohol during his early adulthood, Sequoyah turned his life around and became a fine silversmith and, eventually, a scholar. About 1809 he began work on a written Cherokee alphabet from pictorial symbols, which later evolved into a syllabary (a written alphabet based on syllable sounds) utilizing Greek, Hebrew, and English characters. Although his work was originally rejected by disbelieving tribal leaders, Sequoyah successfully demonstrated his system to the Cherokee tribal council, who formally adopted it in 1821.

A visit to a branch of the Cherokee in Arkansas in 1824 enabled Sequoyah to send written messages back to the eastern Cherokee, prompting thousands of Cherokee men, women, and children to learn to read and write in their own language within a matter of months. The first Native American newspaper, the "Cherokee Phoenix," began publication in 1828. Sequoyah's remarkable achievements made him a respected educator and tribal leader until his death in 1843, and a living monument—the giant California redwood—was named Sequoia in his honor.

voice and leadership. It would soon break apart completely.

In Tennessee, North Carolina, and Georgia, the territory of the Cherokee was in constant danger of being swallowed up by land-grabbing settlers on their way west, who fought with Cherokees off and on for years until the mid-1790s, when Tennessee became a state. The lands of the Choctaw and Chickasaw, in present-day Mississippi, were in no real danger from white settlers for about 20 years after the Revolution. When President Thomas Jefferson enacted the Louisiana Purchase in 1803, however, things changed drastically for the four main Southeastern tribes, and the floodgates opened to unlimited expansion by settlers into the new Louisiana Territory and points west, regardless of what the treaties said.

## AMERICA MOVES WESTWARD

With the Louisiana Territory—land that France had turned over to Spain in 1762, later received back, and then sold to the United States in 1803—now in American hands, settlers poured westward from the confines of the young nation on the Atlantic seaboard. As traders and settlers moved their goods down the rivers and streams of the territory and returned home, they passed through fine country that had belonged to Native Americans for centuries. This was land the settlers wanted—and in many cases, they simply took it. Treaties smoothed the settlers' way. Cherokee lands had been reduced through treaties by more than 50 percent between 1777 and 1809, and white settlers in Tennessee, for example, eventually outnumbered the Cherokee 15 to 1.

In the face of this grave challenge, Southeastern Indian leaders sought to stem the tide of white expansion in whatever ways they could, through legal, legislative, and, when all else failed, military means. In 1809, for instance, Cherokee tribal representatives asked President Thomas Jefferson about his idea for an Indian Territory west of the Mississippi—a plan that was eventually used years later, in what would ultimately become the state of Oklahoma.

Another, more direct approach to preserving Indian lands—united, armed resistance—was preferred by a number of Southeastern leaders in various tribes. The most famous, if not successful, of these visionaries was the great Shawnee

▲ Menewa (c. 1765–1865) was a Creek chief and military leader of the Red Sticks during the Red Stick War of 1813–14. Strongly opposed to whites, Menewa fought against the removal of his people from their ancestral lands to Indian Territory in 1825. This portrait of him dates to 1838.

chief Tecumseh. Although his home was among the Shawnee in Ohio, Tecumseh (and his twin brother, known as the Shawnee Prophet) was part Creek and sought to unite all Indians against a common enemy—the United States. From about 1800 to 1811, Tecumseh traveled throughout the country seeking support for his Indian Confederacy. He appealed to the leaders of the Choctaw (Pushmataha), Chickasaw (the Colbert brothers), Cherokee, and Creek to unite against white expansion, but most were unwilling to make war on the increasingly stronger United States. In 1811, while Tecumseh was away, his forces, led by his brother, were defeated by William Henry Harrison at their village of Tippecanoe, and the movement was broken. Tecumseh joined the British in the War of 1812, and his dream of an Indian Confederacy died with him in battle.

Of the Southeastern leaders who did favor military action against the United States, one of the most prominent was Menewa, a leader of the anti-American Creek faction called the Red Sticks, who attacked Alabama's Fort Mims in 1813, starting the Red Stick War. Instead of uniting the Southeastern tribes, however, the Red Sticks' attacks prompted a counterattack by the U.S. Army and Indian warriors from all four major Southeastern tribes led by General Andrew Jackson at Horseshoe Bend in 1814. This major U.S. victory broke the Creek Confederacy, forcing the Creek to surrender about 20 million acres of land in Alabama, much of which once belonged to tribes whose warriors fought beside Jackson at Horseshoe Bend. Many of the Creek later moved south to Florida and became part of the tribe that, over the next 40 years, would come to represent Native American resistance in the Southeast—the Seminole.

In the two decades following the Red Stick War and the scattering of the Creek, the remnants of that nation and the other Southeastern tribes made great strides to educate their people, be-

# RED EAGLE

An engraving of the 1814 interview between Andrew Jackson and William Weatherford, also known as Red Eagle (c. 1780–1822), the courageous Creek war chief whom Jackson defeated in the Battle of Horseshoe Bend that year. Weatherford and other Creek leaders, including Menewa, were inspired to resist the U.S. Army by the great Shawnee chief Tecumseh. They inflicted heavy casualties on U.S. forces at Fort Mims and Horseshoe Bend but in the end were overwhelmed by Jackson's troops. Upon surrendering his troops—and nearly 20 million acres of Creek lands in Alabama—Weatherford expected to be executed, but Jackson pardoned him on the provision that he work for peace. Weatherford agreed and Jackson, surprisingly, kept his word, too. He granted the Creek women and children safe conduct and allowed Weatherford to return to his home as an advocate for peace between Indians and whites. Red Eagle died peacefully in 1822, several years before Jackson and the U.S. government cleared the Creek from their remaining lands and sent them to Indian Territory across the Mississippi.

coming strong, self-governing nations even as their lands were being systematically stolen from them. In time, these nations—the Creek, Chickasaw, Choctaw, Cherokee, and Seminole—would become known as the "Five Civilized Tribes." But in just a few short years, they would be uprooted from their ancient lands forever.

## THE TRAIL OF TEARS

Remarkably, this period of great tribal growth for the Southeastern nations was also a time when the U.S. government was planning to rid itself of its "Indian problem" east of the Mississippi by forcibly "removing" the Native Americans remaining in the Southeast to Indian Territory (today, Oklahoma). Andrew Jackson, who more than anyone represented the American "frontier spirit" and its mission of clearing the country of Indians, was elected president in 1828. The Indian Removal Bill was adopted into law in 1830; although it didn't authorize enforced removal of the Indians from their lands, it did give the president power to initiate land exchanges with Indian nations living inside states or territories, meaning the five Southeastern nations—the Chickasaw, Choctaw, Cherokee, Creek, and Seminole. These land exchanges effectively gave the government the authority to strip the Indian nations of their ancestral lands and move their entire populations west of the Mississippi River.

Beginning in 1831, the Southeastern Native Americans were driven from their homelands to areas in the Indian Territory to which they were assigned, by tribe, before their departure. The Choctaw were first, and the others soon followed. The Removal, as it was officially called, went on for years, as each nation signed a separate treaty of removal. The people were forced to move on foot, often in the dead of winter, with insufficient clothing and food. Cholera struck each summer from 1831 to 1836. In 1832, the Creek were literally driven from their homes, and many were left to starve in the swamps nearby. Only the Chickasaw, who left in 1837, were able to bring along a good percentage of their belongings and horses.

In 1838 and 1839, the Cherokee—who would not sign a treaty after President Jackson refused to execute a Supreme Court decision condemning Georgia's treatment of the tribe—were forcibly removed by the U.S. Army under a false treaty. The Cherokee suffered the most of all the tribes during the Removal, and nearly one-fourth

▲ Osceola (c. 1804–38) was a great Seminole leader who came to prominence by leading badly outnumbered forces in a successful guerilla campaign against the U.S. Army in the Second Seminole War. Tricked into agreeing to a ceasefire under a flag of truce in 1837, he was captured and died in prison the following year.

of the tribe's population died on the way to Indian Territory.

Small bands of Cherokee took refuge in mountainous areas of North Carolina and emerged decades later as the Eastern Cherokee. Some Choctaw also managed to cling to their native Mississippi lands, and remain there today. The Southeastern nation that most successfully resisted removal, however, was the Seminole, who along with the smaller Miccosukee tribe fought the U.S. Army off and on for decades.

## THE SEMINOLE NATION RESISTS

The resistance of the Seminole nation of Florida to the policies of the U.S. government began long before the Removal of the 1830s. When the Creek nation was broken following Andrew Jackson's

▲ The tenacious Seminole chief Holata Micco, better known as Billy Bowlegs (c. 1810–59). A skilled warrior, Bowlegs fought the U.S. Army off and on during the Second and Third Seminole Wars, between 1830 and 1858.

victory at the Battle of Horseshoe Bend in 1814, many Creek moved south from Georgia to join their Seminole and Miccosukee cousins in Spanish Florida, and the Seminole population doubled. In 1817, General Jackson used border disputes between the Seminole and Georgian settlers as an excuse to invade Seminole country in Florida, and the First Seminole War was underway. Hostilities continued until Spain, under military pressure from the United States, sold Florida in 1819, and Seminole territory officially became a U.S. territory in 1822.

Incidents between bands of Seminole and the U.S. Army continued through the early 1830s. By this time, General Jackson had become President Jackson, and removal of some Southeastern tribes had already begun. While some Seminole leaders

agreed to removal terms, others resisted; one of them, Osceola, was imprisoned but was released on a promise to support the removal. Instead, Osceola organized a strong Seminole resistance force and launched the Second Seminole War in 1835.

Along with Coacoochee (also known as Wild Cat), another famed Seminole warrior, Osceola carried out a successful guerrilla campaign against far superior numbers of U.S. troops in a long, costly war until 1837, when he was imprisoned under a flag of truce by an American general who called for a peace conference. Osceola died in prison the following year. Although his guerrilla forces continued to fight, Osceola's death marked the beginning of the end of the Seminole resistance. Removal and resistance continued, however, until 1042, when American troops gave up trying to root the remaining Seminole out of the Florida swamps.

Nearly a decade and a half after most of the Seminole tribe had been removed to Indian Territory, the U.S. Army tried again, in the mid-1850s, to clear the new state of Florida of Seminole and Miccosukee Indians. But even in the Third Seminole War, which ended in 1858 with the forced removal of some 165 Seminole (mostly women and children), the army was unable to dislodge the remaining Indians from the Everglades. In the 20th century, both the Miccosukee and Seminole peoples remaining in Florida have become incorporated tribes—legally recognized corporate entities—and now own and operate reservations and businesses. The Florida Seminole tribe signed a peace treaty in 1934 and was incorporated in 1957. The Miccosukee, however, who became incorporated as a tribe in 1961, have never signed a treaty; technically, at least, they are still at war with the United States.

## FAREWELL TO ANCIENT LANDS

For the most part, the Southeastern Native Americans after the Removal were Southeastern in name only. The "Five Civilized Tribes," however, thrived—to the extent that a people can thrive under such conditions of duress—in Indian Territory. In fact, the tribal governments of the Chickasaw, Choctaw, Seminole, Cherokee, and Creek developed such strength in the Indian Territory during the second half of the 19th century that there was a strong possibility of the establishment of an all-Indian state. Called Sequoyah,

▲ This photograph shows representatives from 34 Native American nations, gathered for a conference at the Creek Council House in Indian Territory (later to become Oklahoma) in 1880.

after the great Cherokee scholar, the proposed state met its end in 1906, after oil was discovered in the Indian Territory. Like so many times before, once white Americans discovered the value of an Indian possession, it ceased to be an Indian possession. The Indian Territory became the state of Oklahoma in 1907. After the discovery of oil, so many non-Indians had moved into the former Indian Territory that the new state of Oklahoma's thousands of Native Americans made up less than six percent of the total population.

The Five Civilized Tribes, and the remnants of all the other original Southeastern peoples— like virtually all other Native American nations today—live either on tribal reservations or as part of the general population of Americans. Their societies still thrive, even after centuries of abuse; their ceremonies, songs, traditions, religion, and—most of all—their spirits live on.

## THE TWENTIETH CENTURY

With the approach of the 21st century, it is interesting to note what the past 100 years have

meant to the Native Americans, including those who originally lived in the Southeastern United States. At the close of the 1800s, the U.S. government had succeeded in driving most of the continent's Native American tribes out of their ancestral lands and onto reservations. Although some tribes of the Plains and the Southwest continued scattered resistance to the army at the turn of the century, the so-called Indian Wars were effectively over, with the U.S. victorious.

The original Southeastern Indian nations, including the Five Civilized Tribes, had been long established in Indian Territory by 1900. These tribes had grown strong again as individual nations and looked forward to establishing an all-Indian state in the Indian Territory. But after the discovery of oil and the eventual statehood of Oklahoma dashed hopes for an Indian state of Sequoyah, the Southeastern tribes once again lost

▲ A Native American hero: Lieutenant Ernest Childers, a Creek, receives congratulations from General J. L. Devers after being awarded the Congressional Medal of Honor for heroic action in Italy in World War II.

a large amount of tribal land through various agreements. Today, most Indian land in Oklahoma is privately, rather than tribally, owned.

Reservation life for Native Americans has been described as a "culture of poverty," and during the years preceding World War II this description was especially accurate. The average reservation had poor land for raising crops and animals, no industry, and suffered from indifferent government policy, leading to an extremely low standard of living for Native Americans. In the post-war years, however, public awareness of the lack of employment, education, and opportunity for Native Americans has brought some change for the better. In the 1950s and 1960s, many Southeastern tribes—both in Oklahoma and the few left in their native region—began to organize and incorporate themselves, becoming a vital part of their local economies.

In 1961, a conference of Indian tribes drafted a Declaration of Indian Purpose, which explained the need for tribes to retain their own lands. Along with officials of the modern Five Civilized Tribes now based in Oklahoma, the conference was attended by representatives of the Alabama Creek, the Mississippi Choctaw, the North Carolina Lumbee and the Eastern Cherokee, the Florida Seminole, and the Florida Miccosukee. And in 1968, a new organization was formed among the tribes remaining in the Southeast: the United Southeastern Tribes of American Indians, Inc., consisting of the Cherokee, Choctaw, Miccosukee, and Seminole nations.

This organization and others like it continue to strive for the rights of Native Americans, whose standard of living is still among the lowest (and unemployment rate among the highest) of any ethnic group in the United States. With the help of such groups, the Indian peoples still remaining in the Southeast—including the Lumbee, Catawba, Cherokee, Choctaw, Seminole, Creek, and others—might someday begin to enjoy the same standard of living as those who now occupy most of their former lands.

In recent years, self-help efforts by the Southeastern tribes have helped provide employment and economic growth. The Eastern Cherokee, for example, attract many tourists every year to their beautiful reservation in the Great Smoky Mountains of western North Carolina. Tribe members present a play about their history called *Unto These Hills* and perform traditional dances. Crafts produced by workers at shops on the

▲ Although Native Americans still have one of the lowest standards of living among American minority groups, some Indian nations are achieving greater prosperity under strong tribal and business leadership. One such Southeastern Indian leader is Chief Phillip Martin of the Mississippi Band of Choctaw Indians. Under Martin's leadership, the Mississippi Choctaw opened the first of five tribally owned industrial plants in 1979 and have since become one of the largest employers in the state of Mississippi.

reservation are sold all over the world. In addition, the Cherokee operate a lumber mill and motels. The Choctaw of Mississippi, under the leadership of their chief Philip Martin, have become the eighth-largest employer in the state; this tribe is an outstanding example of how Native Americans can successfully become part of modern life.

The struggle is far from over. The Lumbee of North Carolina today continue to fight for federal recognition of their tribal status. The Catawba of South Carolina, who since 1962 have not been recognized as a tribe by the U.S. government, continue to press their land claims. On a more positive note, the Trail of Tears was designated a National Historic Trail in 1987.

The Southeastern Native Americans still persevere and continue to live productive lives and observe their unique traditions on and off the reservation, both in their native lands and in their adopted homes west of the Mississippi.

# MODERN LIFE

\* \* \* \* \* \* \* \* \* \* \* \* \*

## PRESERVING THE PAST

▼ A crew of archaeologists working at an excavation of one of several ancient Indian culture sites in the state of Tennessee.

\* \* \* \* \* \* \* \* \* \* \* \* \*

# CHEROKEE HERITAGE

▶ The Eternal Flame of the Cherokee Nation in Red Clay, Tennessee, is a memorial to those Cherokee men, women, and children who suffered and died on the Trail of Tears— the Removal to Indian Territory— in 1838 and 1839. It also commemorates the reuniting of the few Cherokee bands who remained in the East with the Cherokee Nation that was forced to move.

◀ The printing shop where the first Native American newspaper, the "Cherokee Phoenix," began publication in 1828 is preserved in New Echota, Georgia.

▼ The comfortable home of Cherokee leader Joseph Vann is preserved today as a landmark in Georgia.

# CRAFTS TODAY

\* \* \* \* \* \* \* \* \* \* \* \* \* \*

◀ A dish is carved from wood by a Cherokee man at Oconaluftee Village in Cherokee, North Carolina.

▶ At Oconaluftee Indian Village in Cherokee, North Carolina, a Cherokee woman creates beautiful beadwork in the traditional style.

▼ A Miccosukee woman removes bark from a cypress tree at Shark Valley Indian Village in Everglades National Park, Florida.

✳ ✳ ✳ ✳ ✳ ✳ ✳ ✳ ✳ ✳ ✳ ✳

# POWWOWS

✶ ✶ ✶ ✶ ✶ ✶ ✶ ✶ ✶ ✶ ✶ ✶ ✶ ✶

◀ The face of this Native American dancer at a festival in Tennessee displays the concentration necessary for such a performance.

▼ An exciting and colorful Creek ceremonial dance is performed by dancers of the Poarch Band of Creek Indians in Alabama.

✶ ✶ ✶ ✶ ✶ ✶ ✶ ✶ ✶ ✶ ✶ ✶ ✶ ✶

# INDEX

# PICTURE CREDITS

Alabama Bureau of Tourism and Travel: 23 bottom, 94 bottom; William H. Allen, Jr.: 70; American Museum of Natural History: 16, 31, 32 right, 35, 37 left and right, 52, 55, 57, 59, 60, 61, 63, 75; Cherokee Historical Association: 24, 92; Denver Museum of Natural History, Department of Anthropology: 27 (3), 46, 47, 69 top and bottom; Richard Day: 20 bottom; Effigy Mounds National Monument: 11; Everglades National Park: 19 bottom, 93 bottom; Florida Department of Commerce: 3; Florida State Archives: 54, 56 right, 74; Georgia Department of Industry and Trade: 90 top and bottom; Great Smoky Mountains National Park: 43 bottom; Joseph and Arlene Johannets: 22 bottom; Library of Congress: 12, 13, 14, 26, 28, 36, 40, 58, 64, 76, 78, 82, 85; The Lost Colony/Walter V. Gresham III: 51; Mississippi Band of Choctaw Indians: 62, 88; Mound City Group National Monument: 23 top; Museum of the American Indian: 9 left and right, 22 top, 42, 43 top, 44, 45, 48, 66, 67, 68, 81; National Archives: 6, 29, 30, 33, 38, 84, 86, 87; North Wind Picture Archives: 34, 56 left; Jack Olson: 41 top; George Rhodes: 20 top; Eda Rogers: 17; Sylvia Schlender: 53; C. M. Slade: 21; Tennessee Tourist Development: 8, 10, 32 left, 41 bottom, 65, 71, 72, 89, 91, 94 top; Connie Toops: 39, 93 top; George Wuerthner: 18, 19 top.